DODD, MEAD WONDERS BOOKS

*Wonders of the Mosquito World by Phil Ault*
*Wonders of the World of Bears by Bernadine Bailey*
*Wonders of Animal Migration by Jacquelyn Berrill*
*Wonders of Animal Nurseries by Jacquelyn Berrill*
*Wonders of the Monkey World by Jacquelyn Berrill*
*Wonders of the Arctic by Jacquelyn Berrill*
*Wonders of the Woods and Desert at Night by Jacquelyn Berrill*
*Wonders of the World of Wolves by Jacquelyn Berrill*
*Wonders of Alligators and Crocodiles by Wyatt Blassingame*
*Wonders of a Kelp Forest by Joseph E. Brown*
*Wonders of Rattlesnakes by G. Earl Chace*
*Wonders of the Pelican World by Joseph J. Cook and Ralph W. Schreiber*
*Wonders Inside You by Margaret Cosgrove*
*Wonders of the Tree World by Margaret Cosgrove*
*Wonders of Your Senses by Margaret Cosgrove*
*Wonders of Geese and Swans by Thomas D. Fegely*
*Wonders of Wild Ducks by Thomas D. Fegely*
*Wonders Beyond the Solar System by Rocco Feravolo*
*Wonders of Gravity by Rocco Feravolo*
*Wonders of Mathematics by Rocco Feravolo*
*Wonders of Sound by Rocco Feravolo*
*Wonders of the World of the Albatross by Harvey I. and Mildred L. Fisher*
*Wonders of Sponges by Morris K. Jacobson and Rosemary K. Pang*
*Wonders of the World of Shells by Morris K. Jacobson and William K. Emerson*
*Wonders of Magnets and Magnetism by Owen S. Lieberg*
*Wonders of Measurement by Owen S. Lieberg*
*Wonders of Animal Architecture by Sigmund A. Lavine*
*Wonders of the Bat World by Sigmund A. Lavine*
*Wonders of the Bison World by Sigmund A. Lavine and Vincent Scuro*
*Wonders of the Cactus World by Sigmund A. Lavine*
*Wonders of the Eagle World by Sigmund A. Lavine*
*Wonders of the Fly World by Sigmund A. Lavine*
*Wonders of the Hawk World by Sigmund A. Lavine*
*Wonders of Herbs by Sigmund A. Lavine*
*Wonders of the World of Horses by Sigmund A. Lavine and Brigid Casey*
*Wonders of the Owl World by Sigmund A. Lavine*
*Wonders of the Spider World by Sigmund A. Lavine*
*Wonders of the Dinosaur World by William H. Matthews III*
*Wonders of Fossils by William H. Matthews III*
*Wonders of Sand by Christie McFall*
*Wonders of Stones by Christie McFall*
*Wonders of Gems by Richard M. Pearl*
*Wonders of Rocks and Minerals by Richard M. Pearl*
*Wonders of Barnacles by Arnold Ross and William K. Emerson*
*Wonders of Sea Gulls by Elizabeth Anne and Ralph W. Schreiber*
*Wonders of Hummingbirds by Hilda Simon*

# *Wonders of*
## *Geese and Swans*

THOMAS D. FEGELY

ILLUSTRATED WITH PHOTOGRAPHS AND LINE DRAWINGS

DODD, MEAD & COMPANY
NEW YORK

To Mom and Dad

## ACKNOWLEDGMENTS

It would have been impossible to do a book of this sort without the help and cooperation of others. Special thanks to Bea Boone of the Audio-Visual Department, U.S. Fish and Wildlife Service; Bill Julian, Manager, Blackwater National Wildlife Refuge; Clark G. Webster, Manager, Remington Farms; Jim Vallone, waterfowl collector, and others who have provided photographs or information.

Range maps were adapted by Mike Markowitz from "Waterfowl Tomorrow." Line drawings also by Mike Markowitz.

*Illustration Credits:* Mike Markowitz, 10, 35 (top), 42, 61, 65, 69, 73, 77 (top), 81, 85, 92; Leonard Lee Rue III, 86; United States Department of the Interior, National Park Service Photo, 38; United States Fish & Wildlife Service, Department of the Interior, 20, 22, 26, 28, 31, 37, 39, 40, 44, 67, 93; Clark G. Webster, Remington Farms, 54, 56. All other photographs are by Thomas D. Fegely.

*Frontispiece: The future of our waterfowl heritage depends on how well we manage today's populations and how much we have profited from past mistakes.*

Library of Congress Cataloging in Publication Data

Fegely, Thomas D
    Wonders of geese and swans.

    Includes index.
    SUMMARY: Introduces the physical features, habits, and behavior of the swans and geese of North America.
    1. Geese—Juvenile literature.   2. Swans—Juvenile literature.   3. Birds—North America—Juvenile literature.   [1. Geese.   2. Swans]   I. Title.
QL696.A52F42     598.4'1     75-38360
ISBN 0-396-07307-7

# *Introduction*

One fine March day in 1940, ". . . *at about 7 A.M., a flock of* [Canada] *geese flew over Riverside Farm, Parkton, Maryland. The formation was a perfect V, with the leader possibly four feet in front of the next goose. The count of one string numbered 55. Truly a beautiful sight.*" Thus my notes recorded my introduction to the wonders of geese and their cousins, the swans. What mental images of their far-north nesting grounds that sight of migrating Canada geese stimulated in my mind!

Is there a man alive who, unless he has a heart of stone, does not thrill to the sound and sight of geese or swans on the wing? They are truly magnificently majestic birds. What they lack in the spectral colors of their near-relatives, the ducks, they make up in nobility.

While populations of swans and some geese, such as snow geese and whitefronts, are lower today than before the white man's arrival on this continent, there are now more Canada geese in North American than ever before in recorded history. Because of the Canada goose's sagacity, family fidelity and guardianship, and ready ability to adjust to changing conditions, he has prospered from the white man's agriculture. While agriculture has taken over much of the former duck-producing prairie wetlands, alteration of the vast, goose-producing tundra of the far north has been minimal. And on the wintering grounds of the Canada goose, at least in the eastern half of the United States, things have improved.

Probably the single factor that contributed most to the increase in Canadas was the advent of the mechanical cornpicker. Because the farmer was then enabled to pick corn faster, he could produce more and so began increasing the amount he planted. And because the mechanical picker spilled some of the corn as it picked, it left a bountiful supply of

5

food scattered on the ground. Canada geese gradually adapted to feeding on this waste corn and, seemingly, this supplementary food aided in returning them to their breeding grounds in a more productive condition.

In recent years, whistling swans have adapted to feeding in fields on the upper part of Maryland's Eastern Shore. A noticeable intensification of field feedings occurred coincidentally with the destruction of aquatic plants in the upper Chesapeake Bay as a result of excessive amounts of fresh water and silt dumped by runoff from Hurricane Agnes in 1972.

Appreciating the swans and geese—for their ability to adapt to ever-changing conditions in order to survive, for their idiosyncrasies that provide for successful adaptation, and for their grandeur and fascination —comes more readily with better knowledge of each species. In the following pages of this book, Thomas Fegely gives us, in an interesting and easy-to-read manner, an insight into each species and subspecies as to their distribution, life history, peculiarities and relationship, one to the other.

I enjoyed this venture into the *Wonders of Geese and Swans*. I trust you will, too.

*Clark G. Webster*, Manager
Wildlife Management
Remington Farms

# Contents

INTRODUCTION *by Clark G. Webster*      5

1. SWANS AND GEESE—SCIENTIFICALLY SPEAKING      9

2. PHYSICAL FEATURES      11
   *Size and Weight; Plumage and Coloration; Molting; Sound Production; Sight and Hearing; Legs and Feet; Bill Structure; Hybrids; Longevity; Hazards*

3. HABITS AND BEHAVIOR      21
   *Displays; Feeding; Mating Habits; Nesting; Eggs; Care of Young; Migration; Speed of Flight; Flight Formations*

4. NORTH AMERICA'S SWANS      34
   *The Past 300 Years; Trumpeter Swan; Whistling Swan; Mute Swan*

5. NORTH AMERICA'S GEESE      50
   *Species and Subspecies; Canada Goose; Large Canada Geese—Giant, Western, Atlantic, Todd's, Dusky, Vancouver; Small Canada Geese—Cackling, Richardson's, Taverner's, Aleutian, Lesser; Snow Goose—Lesser, Greater; White-fronted Goose—Common, Tule; Brant—American, Black; Ross' Goose; Emperor Goose; Barnacle Goose*

6. SWANS, GEESE, AND MAN      91
   *In Earlier Times; Management and Control; For the Future*
   BIBLIOGRAPHY      95
   INDEX      96

*Even though ducks (bottom right), geese (bottom left), and swans (left) vary greatly in size and appearance, they share certain broad family characteristics.*

# 1. Swans and Geese —Scientifically Speaking

Members of the family Anatidae—ducks, geese, and swans—come in a variety of sizes and colors. From the tiny green-winged teal duck to the giant trumpeter swan (thirty times larger), some sixty-one species of waterfowl dwell in North America and can be found wherever sufficient food and clean water are available.

Despite the differences in their appearances, all ducks, geese, and swans share certain broad family characteristics. They all have webbed feet, flattened bills, short legs and tails, and rather long necks. Other than that, it would be foolish to generalize, since there are major differences that divide the family into smaller subfamilies.

The ducks are placed scientifically in the subfamilies Anatinae (surface-feeding ducks), Nyrocinae (diving ducks), Merginae (mergansers), Erismaturinae (ruddy ducks), and Dendrocygninae (tree ducks). Ducks are generally smaller than swans and geese and have much shorter necks. Their lower legs are covered with overlapping scales along the front edge, whereas in swans and geese an array of hexagonal scales covers the front part of the leg.

Compared to the duck subfamilies, the swans and geese are relatively easy to identify and classify. Unlike the many varied

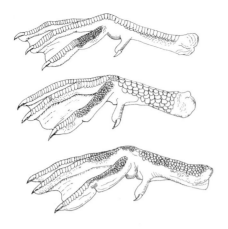

*The scale structure on the fore-legs of ducks (top), geese (center), and swans (bottom) differs.*

colors and physical features of wild ducks, the features of swans and geese are similar enough to one another so that they are only broken down into two subfamilies—the Cygninae (swans) and the Anserinae (geese).

There are seven species of swans distributed throughout the world, although only three of these are found in North America. The whistling swan and the trumpeter swan are native birds, while the mute swan, introduced from Europe, is now common in many parts of the country.

The two native swans are listed as "game birds" in our migratory bird treaties even though no open seasons were declared from 1918 to 1962. In 1962, a limited season on whistling swans was permitted in Utah.

Geese are intermediate in size between the ducks and swans. They are less flattened in shape than the ducks and have longer necks and legs.

Of the thirty-five species of geese found throughout the world, seven of them are found regularly in North America. Canada geese and snow geese are common across the continent, while the white-fronted and Ross' geese have more limited ranges. The brant are found along both coasts, as they prefer the open waters of the oceans and bays. Both the emperor and barnacle geese limit their travels to the far north and venture into the United States only on rare occasions.

# 2. Physical Features

## SIZE AND WEIGHT

The trumpeter swan is North America's largest native member of the waterfowl family. It ranges in length from 60 to 72 inches and in weight averages 22½ pounds (females) to 28 pounds (males). Some individuals weigh over 30 pounds.

Among the geese, the Canada goose is the largest. Strangely enough, the Canada goose is also one of the smallest species in North America. This is explained by the fact that there are eleven subspecies of *Branta canadensis*, which vary in size from the giant subspecies down to the small forms such as the cackling goose. *Branta canadensis maxima*, the giant Canada goose, varies between 10 and 18 pounds in weight. As its scientific name implies, *Branta canadensis minima*, the cackling goose, is much smaller. Its weight averages only 2½ to 4 pounds. The white Ross' goose is about the same size as the cackling goose.

## PLUMAGE AND COLORATION

Unlike the ducks, which have different colors and feather patterns in the males and females, both sexes of swans and geese look alike and lack any iridescent coloration. Although some geese have beautiful feather patterns, few of the large waterfowl are anywhere near as colorful as their smaller web-footed cousins.

Almost all species of swans and geese have considerable amounts of white in their plumage, although in some, such as the Canada geese, the white feathers are restricted to the under-tail *coverts*, the feathers covering the bases of the flight and tail feathers.

Young swans and geese must pass through a stage of immature dress. By the end of their second summer young geese develop their adult feathers, while swans take two or more years to acquire the all-white plumage of maturity.

All waterfowl babies are hatched already dressed in a downy plumage which enables them to take to water almost immediately upon seeing first light. These soft feathers are retained for about three weeks in geese and six weeks in swans. At that time the first true feathers, in the shoulder and tail regions, begin to push out and gradually replace the down.

The *fledgling* period, the time between hatching and flight, varies greatly from one form of swan or goose to another. The tiny Ross' goose and cackling goose, for example, are ready for flight six weeks after hatching. At the other end of the scale, the trumpeter swan is not ready to take to the air until seventeen weeks after leaving the egg.

## MOLTING

Unlike the ducks, which molt twice, swans and geese undergo only one molt each year. This change of feathers takes place after the breeding season and is known as the *postnuptial molt*. At this time the flight, body, and tail feathers are all shed at once and the bird is unable to fly.

A female swan or goose usually begins her molt within two weeks after the hatching of the young. She is, therefore, flight-less for a period of time while tending to her family duties.

*This white-fronted goose is beginning its summer molt.*

About the same time that the female is getting her flight feathers back, the male is losing his. By this delayed timing in feather loss, one of the parents is usually able to defend the brood and itself from predators and intruders.

The period of "grounding" for geese is about four or five weeks, while the swans average six to eight weeks to renew their plumage. By the time that the parents have finished their molt, the young, too, are *fledged* (ready to fly), and the family is able to take off together.

### Sound Production

Nearly everyone is familiar with the honking calls of the Canada geese and the combined voices of hundreds of them passing through the fall sky. Although to our ears the sounds may seem to be a din of meaningless honks, to geese they are a method of communication.

Goose "talk" varies from the familiar *uh-whonk* to a variety of grunts, squawks, and hisses. One scientific study revealed that the Canada goose utters ten different sounds, each one a response to a specific situation.

In geese, sound is produced by inhaling and exhaling air

13

*Swans and geese have monocular vision because their eyes are on the sides of their heads.*

which is temporarily stored in an air sac near the crop. Variations in the size and length of the trachea (windpipe) evidently account for the different calls that geese can make.

The most magnificent voices of all are possessed by the whistling and trumpeter swans, especially the latter. The call of the trumpeter, a hornlike sound, can be heard for more than a mile.

These two swans each have a trachea which is looped inside the breastbone. The combination of this bony chamber plus the length of the windpipe (more than four feet long) provides the swans with their loud, penetrating voices. The difference in the way the windpipe is looped in the breastbone of the two North American swans accounts for the variation in their voices.

The mute swan is actually not "mute" but was so named because it is not nearly as noisy as its cousins. When angry it hisses, and when calling its young it utters a sound which has been compared to the bark of a small dog. The mute swan lacks the long, looped trachea possessed by its North American cousins.

### Sight and Hearing

Although most opinions of the sight and hearing abilities of swans and geese are based on observation, there is little doubt that in both of these senses they are superior to man.

First, the eye placement, on the sides of the head, enables a bird to see what is happening both in front and on the sides without having to move its head. This indicates that the bird is focusing with one eye (*monocular vision*) most of the time, although it can see with two eyes (*binocular vision*) when looking straight ahead.

Like all birds, geese and swans can see colors. Hunters and wildlife photographers frequently dress in camouflage outfits of green, gray, and brown so as not to be detected by the wary birds.

Swans and geese also have an excellent sense of hearing. Resting flocks of geese are frequently observed raising their necks skyward long before the sounds of an approaching flock are audible to human ears.

The ears of all waterfowl are located on the sides of the head in a position similar to that of our ears. They are not visible, however, since there are no external structures and the openings are covered by feathers.

### LEGS AND FEET

The legs and feet of swans are relatively larger than those of geese. The toes of both, however, are joined by webs which enable them to swim rapidly. Three toes on each foot, those which are joined by the web, protrude forward, while the hind toe is slightly elevated and serves no practical purpose.

*The toes of all waterfowl are joined by webs of skin, which enable the birds to swim rapidly.*

The legs of geese are placed more in the center of the body than they are in swans and ducks. They, therefore, are much better walkers and do not "waddle" as much as other waterfowl when moving about on land.

## BILL STRUCTURE

The bills of every member of the Anatidae family have serrations on the mandibles (upper and lower beak parts) called *lamellae*. These toothlike structures fit together to form a strainer, which permits the bird to retain food particles while still enabling excess water to flow from the closed mouth. Since most waterfowl gather some of their food while submerged, this feature is important.

The space between the bill and the eye is called the *lore*. In geese this area is completely covered by feathers; in swans it is bare in adults but covered with feathers in the young and in some immature birds.

The bill itself is covered with a leathery membrane and equipped with a "nail" or horny covering at the tip of the upper mandible. This, along with the bill's natural curvature, serves as a cutting tool with which both types of birds can clip grasses, grains, or whatever food they are after.

In general structure, the swan's bill is high at the base and broad and flattened at the tip. The goose's bill is shorter, narrow in the middle, and tapered toward the end. In some species of geese the mandibles are open on both sides, exposing the lamellae and giving one the impression that the bird is "smiling."

The bill serves as more than just a food-gathering tool. It is also utilized as a "comb" for preening and oiling the plumage to keep it waterproofed. (The oil is pressed from a special gland at the base of the tail.) The bill may also be used as a weapon for biting or striking during courting time and in defense of the young. It also makes possible the movement of nesting materials from one spot to another.

16

*In swans, the lore is bare.*

## HYBRIDS

Waterfowl, more than any other kind of bird, interbreed with one another and produce *hybrids*. Although ducks are well known for this behavior, swans and geese also interbreed with other similar species on occasion.

Many books make reference to a snow goose-blue goose hybrid. Up until recent times it was thought that these two geese were separate species but they are now considered as one. Their plumage differences are known as *color phases*.

Both the black and American brant are also known to crossbreed. Some scientists claim that the brant are actually two different species, while others say that they are merely subspecies and classify them as such. If the latter is true, the young of an American-black brant cross would merely be an inter-race hybrid and not the result of two entirely different species. Similar crosses are known to occur between some of the various subspecies of Canada geese.

Little has been written on hybridization among swans. Since there are only seven species throughout the world and most are of diverse characteristics and ranges, probably few, if any, of these great birds ever interbreed in the wild.

## LONGEVITY

Not very much is known about the maximum ages to which wild swans and geese live. It must be assumed, however, that due to the various dangers and diseases to which wild birds are

17

exposed, they cannot live nearly as long as captive individuals.

The record for longevity seems to be held by the mute swan which has been known to live from 50 to 70 years. Unconfirmed reports list one mute swan as having died at 102 years of age. A captive trumpeter held the record for its kind (32½ years), while a whistler survived in captivity for 19 years.

There are records of a Canada goose having lived 33 years in captivity, and another, possibly even more remarkable, managed to survive for 25 years in a wild state.

The other competitors for the longevity record fall far behind. These include a white-fronted goose (11½ years) and a blue-phase snow goose (10½ years).

## HAZARDS

Although there are many hazards that swans and geese face throughout their lives, a few have been pinpointed and are being studied.

Although more ducks than geese are affected, *botulism* has been responsible for losses of tremendous numbers of waterfowl. The disease is caused by a complex bacteria that infects both birds and mammals. Since geese find less of their food in the

*The mute swan holds the record for longevity.*

marsh mud where this bacterium thrives, they are less likely than ducks to get the disease.

Another disease, *fowl cholera,* has been known to occur in European countries for more than two centuries. Since then it has spread to most parts of the world. Ducks, swans, geese, coots, gulls, shorebirds, and others have died from outbreaks in California and Texas.

*Algae blooms,* strange, uncontrolled growths of toxic algae that form in ponds and lakes, kill any living creature that drinks the water. Since ponds and lakes are the prime areas inhabited by swans and geese, these waterfowl are more likely to be affected than some other animals.

Annual losses due to oil pollution have become serious. Again, ducks seem to suffer most, although brant, being "sea geese," have also suffered losses when leaks occur offshore or from a tanker. Pesticide, mine, and industrial pollutants also take an undetermined toll, either directly or by first eliminating the birds' food supply.

Several types of blood parasites, carried and spread by black flies, infect and kill waterfowl—especially the young. They multiply in a bird's body where they invade the red blood cells, causing severe anemia and finally death.

Various internal parasites, including tapeworms, roundworms, flukes, and the like have been found in geese and swans. External parasites, especially lice, are bothersome to the birds, as are leeches which attach themselves and suck blood. Although they are probably little more than a nuisance to full-grown birds, they may become serious threats to the health of the youngsters.

Feeding waterfowl also pick up spent lead shot from the bottoms of marshes and ponds where hunting has taken place. The bird's digestive juices then dissolve some of the lead and the gizzard becomes partially paralyzed. Since it cannot function to help grind food, the bird starves to death, even though plenty of

19

*Even litter can be a hazard in the life of a goose.*

food may be available. Both swans, particularly whistlers, and geese that feed in wetland shallows have died from lead poisoning. Ammunition manufacturers have developed an iron shot to help combat this problem.

A variety of accidents befall swans and geese, particularly during the spring and fall migrations. Violent storms sometimes injure migrating fowl or blow them out to sea where the birds tire and drown. In flight they may collide with fences, high-tension electrical lines, or bridges, and either injure or kill themselves.

On their northward flights, flocks of whistling swans rest on the Niagara River above the famous falls. In a single instance as many as two hundred are known to have been carried over the falls to meet their death in the rocks and whirlpools below. The tired birds allowed themselves to drift into the rapids and were unable to escape the force of the fast-flowing waters.

Other unusual deaths have occurred when individuals became entangled in the leader material from fishing lines or some other form of litter such as plastic six-pack holders.

Predators and hunters, obviously, take the largest tolls. Specific references to these will be made in subsequent chapters.

# 3. Habits and Behavior

**DISPLAYS**

One of the intriguing aspects of waterfowl watching is the variety of nonvocal displays used to communicate with others of the same and different species.

Most of these displays are instinctive rather than learned. Experiments have shown that youngsters isolated from their parents tend to carry out the same displays and signals as those raised under natural conditions.

Since waterfowl are quite social and typically travel in flocks, preflight behavior patterns can be readily recognized. Canada geese, for example, do much chin-lifting and head-shaking to advertise their conspicuous white face markings to others in the flock. The mute swan signals its imminent take-off by facing into the wind and assuming an alert posture and stiffened, erect neck. Since both swans and geese require room for their running take-offs, these signals, along with their special sounds, are important, especially when danger threatens.

When defending a nest or a brood of young, swans and geese often assume a threat posture. The mute swan is frequently seen lifting its wings, ruffling its feathers, and spreading its tail to make it appear much larger than it really is. The Canada

*This Canada goose gander (left) assumes a threat posture in the defense of the nest.*

goose alternately stiffens and pumps its neck, all the while hissing and shaking its folded wings or holding them outstretched.

At breeding time swans and geese perform a variety of displays that may seem like complete nonsense to a human observer. Paired geese stand side by side, honking loudly in each other's ears, or gracefully curving their necks so that they brush one another. Trumpeter swans face each other with quivering wings, dip their heads beneath the water, then arch their necks in a form of triumph. Besides affirming the bond between mates, these displays also show others of their species that an attachment is formed and warns them to "keep away."

Regardless of the amusement with which we may view the many displays exhibited by swans and geese, these demonstrations are serious to the birds themselves and have an important role in their social structure.

## FEEDING

Like the common "puddle ducks," such as the mallard and black duck, both swans and geese get much of their food by "tipping" in the shallows for vegetable matter. Swans, especially,

*The Canada goose gets some of its food by "tipping."*

are experts at this method of feeding, since their long necks enable them to get down to places where ducks and geese cannot reach.

Although swans do not typically feed on dry land, in recent years whistlers have been feeding considerably in fields in the Chesapeake Bay region. This change in habit has been attributed to the loss of saltwater plants resulting from excessive freshwater runoff and silt buildup from Hurricane Agnes in 1972.

Most geese are regular visitors to grain fields, pastures, and even golf courses where they graze on grasses, seeds, and sprouting grain. Canada geese also do some damage to soybean

*The long necks of swans enable them to get down deep without diving.*

crops and in some areas rely heavily on leftover corn scattered by mechanical cornpickers.

Since the swans and geese of North America are widely scattered, their diets are as varied as the places in which they live. Both types of birds, however, are vegetarians, preferring the tender roots, tubers, stems, and seeds of aquatic plants. Occasionally earthworms, insects, mollusks, and crustaceans are taken by the adults, and the young of both swans and geese seem to rely heavily on this animal matter during their first days.

Like most birds, waterfowl require a certain amount of "grit" in their diets which aids in digestion by grinding the foodstuff into smaller particles. Small amounts of sand and gravel are consumed to aid the gizzard in this grinding process.

The specific diet of each species of swan and goose will be detailed in their life histories.

## MATING HABITS

Swans and geese apparently mate for life. If one of a pair is killed, however, it is believed that the other will seek a mate the following breeding season.

In most species mating takes place before the long migratory flight from the wintering grounds to the summer range. Some

*Geese get much of their food on dry land.*

defer mating until the spring journey is completed.

Geese usually do not breed until their third year (at the beginning of their fourth summer), although it has been estimated that about one-third of all two-year-old Canada geese are paired and breeding. Even though many more two-year-old Canadas and even a few yearlings are paired, this does not necessarily indicate that they will breed that year.

Although little is known of the true breeding ages of swans, it is thought that the whistler and trumpeter do not raise a family until their third or fourth year. Mute swans have reportedly mated at the age of two, but a breeding age of three to as long as five years seems to be more valid.

## Nesting

Unlike most male ducks, which abandon their mates and ignore all nesting duties when incubation begins, swan and goose males remain close by and assist in the protection of the nest and care of the young. Most do not help with incubation of the eggs, however.

Nesting swans stake out territories around their nests, which are always on the ground and near water. The nesting pair will usually tolerate ducks within this area, but geese and other swans they will drive off. Although a female trumpeter might occasionally construct a nest mound of aquatic vegetation, it is more usual for her simply to scrape a depression in the top of a muskrat house and start laying her eggs.

Whistlers are not as particular about their nest sites and have been known to nest a half mile from water. If a small island is available, however, the mated pair will build a mound of mosses, sedges, and grasses one or two feet high. Mute swans, too, build their nests close to water and usually on a bulky pile of available vegetation.

Like the swans, geese like to have a good view of the surrounding countryside and choose such a nesting location when possible. Their nests usually aren't elaborate, and building materials are picked from whatever happens to be available— sticks, reeds, mosses, and the like.

Canada geese are known for using a variety of strange sites for their nesting chores. In the early 1800s, Lewis and Clark reported Canada geese nesting atop cottonwood trees, and biologists have found them in the nests of owls, ospreys, herons, and hawks, even before the original owners had fully abandoned them. Wildlife managers at both public and private refuges provide artificial nest sites such as wire baskets fastened atop sunken trees and wooden platforms or old wash tubs on strong supports offshore in shallow ponds and lakes.

Nest sites appear to be chosen entirely by the female, although the males of both swans and geese tag along behind during the search.

As the eggs are laid, an abundance of swansdown and goose down is usually plucked by the female, from her breast, to line the nest. When she leaves to feed, the down is used to cover the eggs for warmth and as extra insurance against predators.

### Eggs

There is a great variation in the egg size of North American swans and geese.

The mute swan lays the largest egg, 4½ by 3 inches in size, and grayish in color. The trumpeter and whistling swans lay eggs only slightly smaller, although they are usually creamy

*Trumpeter swan eggs about to hatch.*

*Adult geese are defensive and protective of their young.*

white in coloration. As incubation progresses, however, the eggs often take on a brownish tint, the result of staining from the water, mud, and the rotting nesting material.

The giant Canada goose produces dull white eggs 3½ by 2¼ inches in size. Although one would suspect that the small cackling goose would lay eggs proportionately smaller in size, such is not the case. The 2¾- by 1⅞-inch eggs are indeed smaller but do not differ that much, considering that this goose is only about one-quarter the size of its giant relative.

There is considerable variation in the *clutch* size (number of eggs in the nest) and the length of incubation of the various species of swans and geese. These details are covered in the individual life histories.

The eggs of all waterfowl are solidly colored without spots or other markings. The coloration varies from one species to another, however, and ranges from gray through creamy-white to yellow. Goose eggs, too, often become stained during the incubation period.

### CARE OF YOUNG

Anyone who has ever approached a pair of Canada geese with their downy youngsters knows that the adults are extremely

27

defensive and protective. Just as they form a territory around the nest, the parents also establish a sort of "floating territory" around the family group as it moves from place to place.

Although swans are also protective, they do not seem to have the same dedication to raising their young as do the Canada or snow geese. At times, particularly when threatened by humans, trumpeter swans may desert their brood with little or no effort to protect them. Whenever possible, though, they will attempt to lead their offspring to safety among the shoreline plants.

The downy hatchlings of mute swans are famous for their habit of riding on their mothers' backs.

Both the black and American brant, which nest along the far northern shores, lead their young to sea as soon as they are able to travel. White-fronted geese lead their broods into grassy cover when danger threatens. Instinctively they all crouch low as they attempt to escape, making themselves as inconspicuous as possible.

## MIGRATION

All swans and geese are migratory, with the possible exception of the mute swan which is usually satisfied to remain in the region in which it was stocked by man. Small populations of these same swans, or their offspring, have gone wild, however,

*The "legal" flyways.*

*Greater snow geese flying enmasse along the Atlantic Flyway.*

and are no longer confined to one spot. They typically migrate short distances but not nearly as far as the whistling swan. Some, those privately owned, have a portion of their flight feathers clipped so that they have no choice but to stay in one place. In Europe, where the mute swan is a native, wild birds do have established migratory patterns.

Like the ducks, swans and geese make use of the four major flyways that cover the North American continent.

In the late summer and early fall, from their breeding grounds in the Canadian prairie provinces and the far north, hundreds of thousands of southbound waterfowl crisscross paths and finally filter into the four relatively well-defined migratory routes. The following spring, survivors return north along these same paths, timing their arrivals at their nesting areas with the melting snows and thawing ponds and potholes. There they raise their young and spend the summer, until chilling winds and early snows once again drive them southward.

The Atlantic Flyway has more than 32 million acres of wetlands, the great majority of it from Maryland south, in which waterfowl can winter.

The Mississippi Flyway encompasses fourteen states from

29

Minnesota southward to Alabama and covers one-fourth of the area of the entire forty-eight adjoining states. Waterfowl funnel into this flyway from most of the major breeding grounds in Canada, the Great Lakes area, Hudson Bay, and eastern Alaska. More than two dozen kinds of waterfowl use the Mississippi Flyway.

The route of the Central Flyway passes from the pothole country of the Dakotas, Alberta, Saskatchewan, and Manitoba southward through the plains and mountains to Texas. It takes up one-third of the area of all the flyways combined.

The Pacific Flyway lies between the Rocky Mountains and the Pacific Ocean and has the least amount of good waterfowl habitat in the United States.

Several species of waterfowl overwinter in the northern portions of Mexico. Most of these continue their flights across the border after having traveled the Pacific Flyway, although some filter in from the Central and even the Mississippi flyways.

Much has been learned about the migratory patterns of all wildfowl by *banding*—the attachment of identification tags to individual birds. State, federal, and Canadian biologists, along with game management agents, catch ducks, swans, and geese —either in nets or specially designed traps—then place a num-

*Geese migrate at night as well as during the day.*

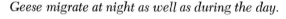

*These Canada geese have been netted for banding.*

bered band on each bird's leg. If the bird is taken by a hunter, found dead or injured, or retrapped in another place, the band is then either removed or the number recorded and sent to the Migratory Bird Populations Station at Patuxent Wildlife Research Center in Maryland.

Each year about 300,000 waterfowl are banded and better than 30,000 bands are recovered. The center's scientists feed the information into electronic computers which store it for later reference and study. Through banding, many of the mysteries of migration are now being answered.

### Speed of Flight

The speed at which a bird can fly has always been of interest to man. There are many variables in judging just how fast a swan or goose can fly, however, since altitude, wind velocity, whether a bird is being chased, and so on, all must be considered.

The normal flight speed of the Canada goose is about forty miles per hour. If it is being chased or is in a hurry for some other reason, it can probably fly at sixty miles per hour maximum. Brant have been clocked in the air at forty-five miles per hour and snow geese at fifty miles per hour.

31

The cruising speed of a trumpeter swan is similar to that of the Canada goose. Due to its size, the swan may seem to be traveling slower. The top speed for these large waterfowl is fifty to fifty-five miles per hour. The whistling swan also travels at about the same speed as the trumpeter.

## FLIGHT FORMATIONS

The great wedges of Canada geese flying overhead in the spring seem to have replaced the robin as the harbinger of the season. There's a scientific reason for the V-formations in which the geese travel, and we can compare it to the same principle used by race car drivers.

A racer will always get as close to the car in front as possible, to take advantage of the draft created by it. The front car tends to "break up" the air and form sort of a vacuum. The rear car, therefore, does not have to battle as much air resistance and can move ahead with less effort.

Down through the years, several types of geese and even some ducks and swans have discovered this same principle. Instead of flying in a straight line, each successive goose flies slightly to the left or right of the one in front of it. They probably do this so that they can see forward. When a large flock congregates, each goose gets in line as described and consequently a V is formed. These wedges vary in size from only a few birds to several hundred.

The lead bird, obviously, is the one that has to work the hardest during a long migratory flight. Therefore, leaders frequently change positions as do other members of the chain. A flock may seemingly break up for a short time, then reassemble again without having slowed down or lost any time. Occasionally two smaller flocks will join together as smoothly as if they had practiced the move many times in the past.

All of the Canada geese migrate in V-formations as do the

32

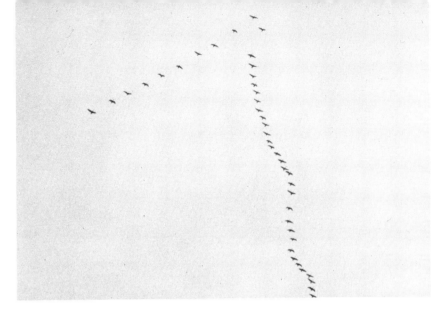

*Most geese migrate in V-formations.*

snow, white-fronted, and Ross' geese. Sometimes these V's are quite loosely formed, with small bands scattered throughout the middle of the wedge. The two species of brant typically fly in long, undulating, curving lines rather than in the typical V.

Flight formations of swans vary greatly, although they, too, may take advantage of V-formation travel at times. Whistlers either form a staggered V or a single diagonal line. Trumpeters migrate in similar patterns, although the V is not as perfected as it is with geese.

On short flights between feeding grounds, both swans and geese travel in irregular formations, especially when the distance does not allow them sufficient time to form.

During migration, it is often necessary for waterfowl to pass above high mountain ranges. Although the maximum altitude at which swans and geese have flown is unknown, whistling swans have been seen from an airplane at eight thousand feet and Canada geese have been spotted at nine thousand feet. Terrain, weather conditions, and length of flight undoubtedly influence the height at which all of these birds fly.

33

# 4. North America's Swans

## THE PAST 300 YEARS

The Migratory Bird Treaty of 1918, between Great Britain and the United States, prohibited the shooting of swans in the United States and Canada. Up until that time both whistling and trumpeter swans, particularly the latter, suffered heavy losses at the hands of man.

Back in the early 1700s, trumpeter swans could be found throughout most of the North American continent. Vast numbers of them wintered as far south as the Gulf of Mexico and along the Atlantic seacoast. They bred from Alaska and northern Canada, south to Iowa and Missouri, and east to Indiana. Great flocks of these birds intermingled with even greater numbers of whistling swans.

As settlers spread across the United States, they exploited many forms of wildlife, including the large and conspicuous swans. Indians cherished the swans for their feathers and their meat, but they also made use of swan bones for tools and jewelry. It was the white man, though, who mercilessly slaughtered the great birds and started their decline.

Swan skins and quills were popular trade items around the turn of the nineteenth century. Artist and naturalist John James Audubon used trumpeter quills for his finest work, declaring

34

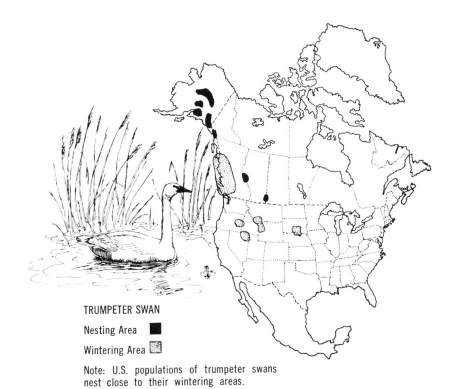

TRUMPETER SWAN

Nesting Area ■

Wintering Area ▨

Note: U.S. populations of trumpeter swans
nest close to their wintering areas.

*Many United States trumpeter swans were introduced into their present
habitats in the West and Midwest.*

that they far surpassed in hardness and flexibility the best steel pens of that time.

Between the years 1823 and 1880, the Hudson's Bay Company bought and sold 108,000 swan skins in London. They were used in the millinery trade for adornment of ladies' garments as well as in the manufacture of powder puffs and down covers.

To the north the Indian hunters killed the adult birds at times when their molts rendered them flightless. Since the young were also unable to fly, they, too, were taken along with the readily available eggs. Because it nested in the same places frequented by early Canadian and border-country trappers, the trumpeter swan was more vulnerable than the whistling swan. By the end of the nineteenth century, the vast flocks of trumpeters had been reduced nearly to extinction. Even though the whistlers also suffered from man's abuses, the killing did not reach the proportions of the trumpeters. Most likely their relative success can be attributed to the fact that they were only available in regions where man lived in the fall and winter. In the spring and summer when they nested, molted, and raised their young, they migrated far to the north where few human predators lived.

Although the Migratory Bird Treaty of 1918 finally outlawed the hunting of swans, it appeared to be too late to do any good. In 1933 biologists found only sixty-six of the once-abundant trumpeter swans in the United States. A few years later, though, the Red Rock Lakes National Wildlife Refuge was established in the Centennial Valley of southwest Montana. Here the beginnings of the trumpeter's return were initiated and the swans are still increasing today.

TRUMPETER SWAN—*Olor buccinator*

By December of 1968, the trumpeter's population had swelled to over five thousand individuals. Today there are enough of

36

*The trumpeter's nest may measure five feet across.*

these majestic birds that they are no longer on the United States Fish and Wildlife Service's "endangered species" list.

With the establishment of the Red Rock Lakes National Wildlife Refuge, a few surviving trumpeters thrived under the protection and privacy offered them. As their populations increased, some of the birds were captured and moved to other refuges in Oregon, Nevada, and Wyoming. Yellowstone National Park in Wyoming has also maintained breeding trumpeters from the times of their persecution until today.

The trumpeter swan's Latin name was derived from its famous hornlike call. *Olor* means simply "swan" and is shared by several others in the family. The species' name, *buccinator*, means "trumpeter" and is owned exclusively by our North American bird.

The trumpeter's nest, often built atop a muskrat lodge, may measure five feet across when completed. Like miniature steam shovels, some swans build mounds of vegetation in which to lay their eggs, while others simply scoop out a depression atop the lodge and the female immediately gets down to the chore of egg-laying.

The average clutch is three to seven eggs, although five or six is typical and as many as nine have been recorded. The *pen*, as all female swans are called, incubates her eggs for twenty-eight to thirty-two days. During this time she spends many hours preening her white feathers while her mate, known as a *cob*, stays nearby to guard the territory.

When a young swan, called *cygnet* (pronounced SIG-nit), is ready to hatch, it breaks its way through the heavy 1/25-inch thick shell by means of an egg tooth. This "tooth" is actually a sharp point at the tip of the upper mandible and is later lost.

In the United States, hatching normally occurs during the third or fourth week in June. Farther north it probably occurs later as summer advances. Biologists have discovered that there is only a one-half to two-thirds hatching success. Infertile eggs and the death of the embryos account for most of the losses, although little is known of the causes of these failures.

Because pecking their way from the heavy shell is hard work, and because the hatchlings are covered with a coat of wet down, the tiny birds spend their first few hours of life resting. Shortly thereafter, the *precocial* youngsters begin to walk and swim and are even able to feed themselves. (Precocial birds are those

*While incubating her eggs, a female trumpeter tends to the nest and preens her feathers.*

*Young swans are called cygnets.*

covered with down, which can move about and feed shortly after leaving the egg. Unlike the young of herons, songbirds, hawks, and some others which must constantly be cared for and fed for several weeks before leaving the nest, waterfowl are much better developed upon hatching.)

The newly hatched cygnets weigh about seven ounces and are dressed in coats of gray fuzzy down. Protected by the adults, the youngsters move about the territory throughout the day, frequently returning to the safety of the nest where the pen continues to warm them. Nights, cold spells, and rainy periods also find the youngsters sheltered beneath their mother's feathers.

The first few weeks of a young swan's life are its most hazardous. Some become entangled in water plants and drown, others may be trampled by their clumsy parents, and a few fall prey to internal parasites and leeches. Great horned owls, raccoons, golden eagles, and coyotes also take a small toll.

The first foods of the cygnets are primarily aquatic insects and crustaceans. Although the youngsters can dive to escape danger, they typically feed in the shallows and search among the food items stirred from the muddy bottom by their long-necked parents. In four to five weeks the cygnets gradually

39

*Trumpeter swans can cruise at about forty miles per hour.*

change their food from animal to plant matter. In another month or two they feed themselves independently and thrive on the same vegetable matter favored by their parents. Practically all parts of the aquatic plants are devoured, from root to leaf.

Young trumpeters can usually take to the air by about the end of September. Like their parents, they must first "taxi down the runway" like an airplane before getting off the water. In flight they are smooth and graceful, and are soon able to cruise at forty miles per hour with deep, measured strokes of their powerful wings. While flying, the swans' feet and slender necks are extended straight out.

In the Red Rock Lakes-Yellowstone regions, trumpeters are year-round residents. There the waters are naturally heated by the hot springs of the region and the trumpeters find it unnecessary to embark on the hazardous migrations which spelled doom to many of their ancestors. The north-country swans migrate southward into British Columbia where they flock up to spend the cold season. In both of these regions, government rangers supply the trumpeters with thousands of bushels of grain to assure their survival until winter breaks its icy grip and the birds can once again fend for themselves.

40

### Whistling swan—*Olor columbianus*

Even though the vast numbers of whistling swans that thrived in the past are now gone, a comparatively large and stable population still exists. The whistler is the wild swan of North America with which most birdwatchers are familiar.

The whistler closely resembles the trumpeter and it is difficult to distinguish between the two unless one can get a close-up look. The presence of a yellow spot on each lore of the whistler is usually sound enough evidence of its identity, although not all whistlers have this mark. The comparatively restricted range of the trumpeter eliminates the possibility of sighting one in most of the whistler's larger geographic range. This is the only native swan found east of the Mississippi. One recent estimate placed the present population of whistlers at around 100,000.

The whistler is the only swan that has been legally hunted, even though areas, seasons, and bag limits are minimal. In 1962 an experimental season on whistlers was established in Utah. A thousand "one-bird" permits were sold and resulted in the bagging of 320 swans during the first year. The season was con-

*The whistler resembles the trumpeter but is distinguished by a yellow spot on the lores.*

WHISTLING SWAN

Nesting Area ■

Migration Stops ●●●

Wintering Area ▦

tinued in Utah and opened on a limited basis in Nevada in 1969 and Montana in 1970.

Although there are vehement protests against swan hunting, biologists have determined that the open seasons have little, if any, effect on the populations. Hunters, rather than disease and the elements, seem to substitute for the natural deaths that occur in the wild. The one danger lies within the states that also have trumpeter swans, since it is difficult, if not impossible, to readily identify them in flight.

Hunters typically have the preconceived notion that a swan is an easy mark but they are quick to lose this idea. Those who were successful and have eaten swan describe its taste as "delicious" and every bit as tender and tasty as wild goose.

The majority of whistling swans nest north of the Arctic Circle and are scattered widely across the tundra. Along the edge of a lowland pond, a pair of whistlers will construct a massive nest of grasses, mosses, reeds, sedges, and the like. This building material is usually not carried very far but consists of whatever items are within neck-stretching distance. Although the male helps out, the female does the majority of the construction. In some heavily populated breeding areas, due to competition for space, certain nests may be added to each year and the resulting nest may be as much as six feet wide and two or three feet high.

Whistlers begin to lay their eggs in late May or early June, shortly after arrival from the wintering grounds in the south. Two to seven creamy-white eggs may be produced but four or five seems to be the average number. One egg is laid every other day until the clutch is completed. At that time, the pen begins her incubation duty which lasts thirty-five to forty days. The cygnets hatch in late June or early July.

Within hours after breaking out of their eggs, young whistlers are ready to take to water. For the next few weeks, however, the nest is still the center of family activity and the spot to which they return to rest and spend the night.

Cygnets are grayish with pink bills and feet. While the oldsters feed on deep-rooted vegetation, the youngsters search for insects and other invertebrate animal life nearby. Some of these animals are stirred from the bottom mud which the adult swans disturb in their underwater feeding activities. In deep water the adults often "tip up" to reach the submerged morsels. The youngsters are good divers but use this skill only as a form of escape, not for feeding.

Although all swans are primarily vegetarians, whistlers that spend the winter in the Chesapeake Bay region on the borders of Delaware, Maryland, and Virginia supplement their diets of widgeon grass and wild celery with thin-shelled clams and other mollusks.

By mid-September the family group has grown a new set of

*Whistling swan cygnets are grayish with pink bills and feet.*

feathers and the youngsters are making practice take-offs and landings in anticipation of the long migration flight. Occasionally, when a pair mates and raises a brood late in the season, the young will still be flightless when the temperatures drop below freezing. And even though the adults are protective and take good care of their offspring, should the open waters freeze before their flight feathers are grown, some of the youngsters never gain flight and perish on the feeding grounds. Others, suffering from malnutrition, may die from exhaustion during the long southward journey.

Enroute to their winter resorts, large flocks of whistlers may set down temporarily wherever bodies of open water offer them food and safety, regardless of the temperature. Their water-resistant coats, along with a heavy insulating layer of down and fat, seem to keep them comfortable even at 40 degrees below zero.

When migrating, swans often travel in V-shaped wedges, an old experienced cob usually doing the leading. With their necks stretched outward and with steady, slow beats of their wings, the swans travel far above the ground. Often their high-pitched voices will be heard long before they can be seen as mere specks against the sky.

Although they must fly high to cross the summits of certain

44

*The whistler's insulating coat of feathers, down, and fat keeps it warm at freezing temperatures.*

mountains, the exact height of their travels has not been documented. In 1962, an airliner collided with a whistler at six thousand feet, causing the plane to crash. Other whistlers have been seen at eight thousand feet.

The law protects the whistling swan in its winter home and its own wariness and the remoteness of its nesting territory further add to the whistler's safety. The long instinctive flight of the whistler may seem peculiar and needless when compared to the relatively sedentary habits of the trumpeter. Were it not for this characteristic, however, perhaps the numbers of whistling swans would not be as great as they are today.

### Mute swan—*Cygnus olor*

The mute swan is not a native bird. Introduced from Europe and now a common resident of many town and city parks, the mute swan is capable of uttering a bugle-like call and frequently hisses when angry or disturbed.

The mute swan is not quite as large as the trumpeter swan, although an adult's wingspread will exceed seven feet and its weight varies from twenty to thirty pounds. Both close up and

*The mute swan has a bright orange bill with a black "knob."*

at a distance, the mute is readily identifiable from the whistler and trumpeter. Our two wild swans typically carry their long necks stiffly erect, while the mute holds its neck in a graceful S-curve. Furthermore, this "foreigner" has a bright orange bill with a black knob just above the nostrils. The other swans have black bills which are carried straight ahead, while the mute carries its bill pointed downward, probably because of the way it holds its neck.

Mute swans have been residents of royal estates in Europe and the British Isles for hundreds of years. Although many of these are domesticated, there are wild flocks in southern Scandinavia, northern Germany, Denmark, the British Isles, Poland, and parts of Russia and Asia. The wild mute swan's migrations are not as lengthy as the whistler's, but it does leave the colder portions of its breeding range to winter in southern Europe, northern Africa, and southwestern Asia.

Feral (wild) mute swans are quite common throughout England, and because of their beauty have been introduced into ponds, lakes, and rivers throughout most of the world. One recent estimate placed their captive population in Great Britain at about 19,000 birds.

Mute swans were imported into North America in the early 1900s and kept confined on private estates along the lower Hudson River and on Long Island, New York. From these, several feral populations have developed and they now range into Massachusetts, Rhode Island, New Jersey, Maryland, Delaware, Pennsylvania, Michigan, and West Virginia. They may also be found in several other scattered locations throughout the United States.

Like the two native swans, mutes build bulky nests from reeds, sticks, weeds, grasses, and other available vegetation. The nest site may be along the shore of a lake or pond, on an island, or even on a raft of floating vegetation.

One strange feature of a mute swan's nest is that it continues to grow larger throughout the incubation period. Even though the nest may measure as large as five feet long and two feet high, the pen still continues to pick up bits and pieces of nearby vegetation to line the rim.

*Most mute swans are confined, although there are some wild flocks in the East.*

The pen lays one egg every other day until a clutch of four to seven is completed. The blue-gray eggs are larger than those of the trumpeter or whistler, measuring 4½ by 3 inches in size. Both the pen and the cob may take turns incubating the eggs which hatch in thirty-five to thirty-eight days. At times, when both adults are off the nest feeding, the pen covers the eggs with down plucked from her breast. Only when she is satisfied that the cover of swansdown will protect the unhatched eggs from sun, cold, or predators such as crows and gulls will she venture away from the nursery.

Since the eggs are laid at 48-hour intervals, and incubated immediately, they don't all hatch at the same time. Although the downy youngsters will stay in the nest a day or two to dry off and gain strength, the cob will often lead the first-hatched into the water while the pen stays behind to warm the remaining eggs.

Although the mute swan has been domesticated for centuries, captive birds are never really "tame." Where several species of waterfowl live in a confined area, the swan dominates them all. Cats, dogs, and man himself soon learn that an angry swan is not to be tampered with. This is doubly true during the brooding period when the youngsters are still unable to fend for themselves. In England there are recorded incidents of small dogs being dragged into the water and killed by the angry birds.

The cygnets wear sooty gray coats of down. Their small beaks are black and show no indication of the fleshy knob that will develop as they mature.

Mute swans have a distinctive method of brooding their young which seldom occurs in trumpeters and whistlers. The cygnets will frequently crawl onto their mother's back and move under the wings for warmth and protection. At times all that is visible among the pen's white feathers is the head of a curious youngster.

48

*A mute swan takes a nap.*

In addition to water plants, mute swans will eat occasional frogs and fish. The main food of the cygnets consists of insects and other invertebrates, but they soon graduate to a vegetable diet. In captivity, where their diets have to be supplemented, they are fed a mixture of barley, wheat, buckwheat, cracked corn, bread, and crushed dog biscuits. Even in winter they require green food in their diets.

Although adult swans mate for life and there is no need to re-establish new bonds each breeding season, there is considerable threatening and fighting among the young males. The females form attachments when they are a year old but do not lay eggs until their second or possibly their third year.

On windy days the adult swans may be seen using their wing feathers as sails. Raised in an archlike fashion over the back, the wings catch the breeze and effortlessly propel the birds across the pond or lake.

Were it not for the importations of this beautiful bird, many people, particularly easterners, would never get to see a live swan. The mute swans' presence is welcome wherever they have been introduced and especially in places where small flocks have returned to the wild.

# 5. North America's Geese

Prominent among birds which have always held a special attraction and interest for man are the wild geese. Even today, as our lands become more and more industrialized and urbanized, the undulating ribbons of geese calling down from a blue April sky give the promise of warmth and evidence of a more gentle season.

Although their populations have suffered since pre-Colonial days, most of North America's wild geese exist in large enough numbers so that they are in no danger of extinction. Yet, the drainage of wetlands, drought, and the inevitable movement of civilizations has eliminated much prime nesting territory, and man has had to step in to manage the existing wild flocks.

Unlike the swans, geese are present in every state of the Union. Seven species of geese nest and spend the winter on the North American continent. Except for the Canada geese and the snow geese, however, the other five kinds have somewhat restricted ranges and are not commonly seen, except as occasional stragglers, in other parts of the continent.

All of our native geese are artificially classified by wildlife biologists as "game birds." That is, they are hunted for food and sport and their existence depends heavily on scientific management by man. As strange as it seems, the classification

*The Canada goose is common throughout the United States.*

of birds, or even mammals, as "game species" gives them a legal form of protection. When the Migratory Bird Treaty between the United States and Great Britain was drawn up, it provided for the complete protection of songbirds and the management of migratory game birds through controlled seasons. In 1936 a similar treaty was signed with Mexico so that the three countries could share in efforts to preserve this resource that knows no political borders.

Even though all North American geese are considered as game, not all of them are hunted. Some, such as the Ross' goose, are too rare to hunt, while others have restricted ranges. The Canada goose is by far the best known and the one typically sought after by hunters. From year to year waterfowl hunting laws may change within each of the four flyways. The basis for changing these laws regarding bag limits, complete protection of a species, season dates and length, and so on, lies in scientific investigations and surveys carried out by government biologists.

51

## SPECIES AND SUBSPECIES

Every living thing known to man, plant or animal, has a scientific name. Although its common name may vary, the scientific name is the same everywhere throughout the world, regardless of the language spoken. The scientific name is composed of two Latin or Greek words, which indicate genus and species.

The geese, particularly the Canada, snow, white-fronted, and brant, are also broken down into more exact groupings known as *races* or *subspecies*. The third term in the scientific name denotes the subspecies, although each goose may also have a more exact common name. For example, *Branta canadensis interior* is known commonly as the Todd's Canada goose and differs somewhat in range and body features from the other ten subspecies.

## CANADA GOOSE—*Branta canadensis*

To most people, the "wild goose" is the Canada goose. Its range blankets the United States, most of Canada, and parts of Mexico. Throughout its range, the Canada differs greatly in size and slightly in the color of its plumage, but its jet black head and neck with a broad white chin-strap serve to separate it from any of the other wild waterfowl.

No other goose fits the "honker's" color pattern. Besides its striking head and neck feathers, the grayish-brown body, light underparts, and black feet are like no other wild goose. In flight, the upper and lower tail coverts converge to form a white crescent just above the black fan-shaped tail.

All eleven of the Canada goose subspecies look pretty much alike. The grayish-brown bodies of the larger races tend to be a light gray, while the smaller ones are more brown in color. Except for the variations in their overlapping ranges and a few other minor differences, all Canada geese carry on similar life styles.

52

The honker is distinctly an American bird. It is the most widely distributed and best known waterfowl on the continent and at one time or another resides everywhere from secluded backwater marshlands to parks and lakes amid the hustle and bustle of city life.

The goose is a model of domestic faithfulness and dedication. Ordinarily a pair mates for life and only the death of one will urge the other to seek a new partner. As parents, they are rivaled by few other birds when it comes to protecting and raising a family. They will even adopt stray and orphaned young of other Canadas when the occasion presents itself.

Canada geese have a tendency to return to the same breeding grounds on which they were hatched. For some birds the flight is relatively short, while others may have to travel as much as four thousand miles from their wintering places. Unlike ducks, Canada geese fly an arrowlike course. Where the ducks have a tendency to follow coastlines or river routes, the honkers fly above field, forest, and town in their noisy spring and fall excursions. At this time the skies anywhere from Maine to Mexico

*The Canada's jet black neck and contrasting white chin strap make it easy to identify.*

*Canada goose parents are very protective.*

and Washington to Florida might well have a wedge of geese traveling through both night and day. The various races, however, may be common in one or two of the flyways and completely absent from the others.

Since the adults already mated on their wintering grounds, there is no need to undergo the ritual of courtship upon their arrival in the nesting area. The two-year-old *ganders* (males), however, often engage in savage battles with one another over the attentions of an available female. Studies show that only about one-third of these two-year-olds (those birds beginning their third summer) and older raise families, while the yearlings spend the season as "loners."

Upon their arrival at the breeding grounds, it is believed that family groups are still intact. When the mated birds begin their nesting chores, though, they become intolerant of all other geese, including their own young.

As soon as a nest site is established, a territory is set up and guarded vehemently by the gander. The size of the territory varies, depending on the type of cover and the total numbers of breeding pairs present. Records indicate that in some places as many as thirty nests per acre have been found, while in others there has been an average of only one nest per hundred or more acres. Although they strictly forbid the entry of other geese, the tenants are usually tolerant of other birds such as ducks, egrets, and herons.

Marshes, swamps, ponds, lakes, stream and river banks, and even backyard pools will attract nesting geese. The goose selects a suitable location and begins the construction of a bulky nest of mosses, weeds, sticks, reeds, grasses, and any other available vegetation. The gander is only an observer and bodyguard at this time and does not take part in any of the nest-building or incubation duties. When the nest is completed, it may contain several bushels of plant material. Nest size seems to vary proportionately with the size and race of the goose doing the building.

Once the nest is completed, the female immediately gets down to the job of egg-laying. To the south, eggs may be produced as early as the beginning of March, while in the colder reaches of the continent they may not be laid until early June.

The clutch varies in size from two to nine eggs with the average being five or six. They are laid at intervals of twenty-four to thirty-six hours. As each egg is positioned in the nest, the female adds down which is plucked from her breast and belly. This goose down, long known for its insulation qualities in bedding and sleeping bags, provides a soft inner lining which is moved about to cover the eggs when the nest is vacated by the parent. As more down is added throughout the incubation period of four weeks or more, the female develops a bare spot on her breast known as an *incubation patch*. This exposed patch of skin is pressed against the eggs to keep them warm and at an even temperature of about 101 degrees. At intervals, she turns the eggs to expose all sides to the warmth of her body.

In the arctic north, predators constitute a threat to unguarded eggs. Foxes, jaegers, gulls, ravens, crows, mink, and others all

*These Canada geese young are just out of the egg, and will soon be ready to take to the water.*

have a fondness for eggs, as do badgers, magpies, coyotes, skunks, and raccoons in the south. Should the gander spot an egg thief before he has had chance to do his pilfering, however, the defensive goose will most likely drive it away.

As the incubation period nears its end, the parent birds stay close to the nest as if in anticipation of the great event. Then, one by one, the goslings begin to crack through the shell, using the egg tooth on the tips of their tiny black beaks. It may take a day or more for the newcomers to work their way completely out of the shell. The parents offer no aid to them. Even though egg-laying has taken up to a week, all of the goslings hatch out within a 24-hour period. This indicates that incubation probably does not start until the last egg is laid. Quite often there will be a few eggs that do not hatch due to infertility or some other factor.

The precocious goslings are able to run about and swim as soon as they are dry. They look no different than any other species of gosling at this time, as most baby geese have the typi-

56

cal dull yellow down and black legs and bills. The young of the larger races of Canadas weigh 3½ to 4½ ounces, while others are proportionately smaller.

Once the family leaves the nest they do not return to it again for the duration of the season. The vigilant parents lead the goslings to the safety of open water. This may be nearby in most instances while in others the troop may have to travel several miles. If the adults choose to nest in a tree, on the side of a cliff, or in some other high spot, the youngsters must first make a hazardous leap before setting out on their first journey.

During the first weeks of life, goslings are fair game for predators of all types. They are not necessarily easy targets, though, for they are excellent divers. Should a hawk, owl, or gull decide to attack, the goslings will instinctively dive and swim underwater for a distance before resurfacing.

During the entire brood period, from the time that they are downy youngsters right through the latter periods when they resemble miniature versions of their parents, they are well protected. Typically, the entire family is seen walking or floating from place to place, the gander in the lead and the goose behind, with all of the goslings strung out single file in between.

In crowded nesting areas, "gang broods" are sometimes

*After six weeks, the goslings are beginning to show the white cheek patches.*

*After eight weeks, there is little visible difference between parents and young.*

formed numbering anywhere from ten to one hundred goslings with many adults. In the arctic and in other regions where there is plenty of room, this behavior is uncommon.

By the end of the first two weeks of its life, a gosling will have increased its weight four times. Its coloring has changed from tawny yellow to a dirty gray. Small bristled tail feathers also begin to appear.

After another two weeks the tail and wing feathers start to show, and by the time they are six weeks of age, white cheek patches, black neck feathers, and other adult markings are visible. Depending on the race of Canada goose, flight stage may be reached in only six weeks (cackling Canada goose) or it may take as long as ten weeks (giant Canada goose) after hatching. By this time the parents have molted and grown new flight feathers and the entire family is ready for migration.

For the next year or so the family maintains close ties. Mornings and evenings and even in midday they move about together feeding. Since they are essentially grazers, that is, they feed on the ground, large flocks are often seen in grain fields where they are sometimes chased by the farmers. In addition to grains, the Canada will feed on grasses, clover, and a variety of weeds and water plants. Side dishes of grasshoppers, insect larvae, crustaceans, and mollusks are also relished—especially by the goslings. In deep water they will "tip up" to get the submerged food.

When feeding, one or more birds serves as sentinel. A warning call soon brings the others to attention and readies them for a quick take-off. During the hunting season, sentries also maintain their vigilance during both the feeding and resting periods.

As the days shorten, the geese become restless and gather in large noisy flocks. Then one day, along with the changing hues of the autumn leaves, a faint but familiar honking drifts across the countryside. And accompanied by a chill that runs up and down our spines, we see V-shaped flocks against the clear blue sky and know that the wild geese have come back to spend the winter.

Although there is little chance of mistaking a Canada goose for any other kind of bird, it is easy to confuse the eleven sub-

*When feeding, some birds stand sentinel.*

*A flock of honkers set their wings before landing.*

species or races with one another. The greatest variation occurs in the northwestern regions of the continent. Seven races of Canada geese nest in the arctic and subarctic breeding grounds.

Even though biologists have studied the various races of geese for many years, they still do not agree completely on their classification. Generally, though, the authorities feel that the eleven subspecies identified thus far are accurately classified, although future studies may lead to some changes.

There is a gradual change in size and color of the geese from north to south. Birds nesting in the arctic are small, short-necked, and short-billed and become progressively larger in the prairies and forests to the south. The darkest geese occur in the far northwestern coastal regions while those in the interior and northeastern parts of North America are much lighter. Geese found in between these extremes are intermediate in size and color.

From the birdwatcher's and hunter's viewpoint, there are only two types of Canada geese—large and small. The following thumbnail descriptions, therefore, separate the geese into these two broad groups.

## GIANT CANADA GOOSE—*Branta canadensis maxima*

As its name implies, *maxima* is the largest of the eleven races of Canada geese. This bird was thought to have become extinct back in the early 1920s, but in 1960 a biologist working with the Illinois Natural History Survey identified some members of the race in a flock of geese wintering near Rochester, Minnesota. Since then, additional birds have been discovered on refuges in Minnesota, South Dakota, North Dakota, Michigan, and Saskatchewan. Many game breeders in the northcentral states raise the giant Canada and both federal and state conservation agencies stock the birds to reinforce local populations.

The weight of a mature "giant" ranges from ten to eighteen pounds and some even top twenty pounds. Larger birds may have a wingspread exceeding six feet with equally long necks and large broad bills. They are light in coloration with exceptionally large cheek patches.

LARGE RACES OF CANADA GEESE

| POPULATION | SUBSPECIES |
|---|---|
| 1. North Atlantic | Atlantic |
| 2. South Atlantic | Atlantic and Todd's |
| 3. Southeast | Todd's |
| 4. Mississippi Valley | Todd's |
| 5. Eastern Prairie | Todd's |
| 6. Western Prairie | Todd's, Giant, and Western |
| 7. Giant | Giant |
| 8. Great Basin | Western |
| 9. Vancouver | Vancouver |
| 10. Dusky | Dusky |

*A Richardson's Canada goose (left) with a Western Canada goose.*

### WESTERN CANADA GOOSE—*Branta canadensis moffitti*

The western Canada goose is second to the giant Canada in size. A thirteen- to fifteen-pounder is considered large and the average is around eight to ten pounds.

The "westerns'" range is scattered since they live in distinct flocks throughout the West. They breed west of the Continental Divide in British Columbia, northeastern California, northwestern Nevada, eastern Washington, and southcentral Oregon. Others can be found in Utah, Montana, Wyoming, Alberta, and Saskatchewan. In winter they may remain near their nesting areas but some migrate as far south as northern Mexico.

The western Canada goose's population is presently estimated at about 115,000 birds.

### ATLANTIC CANADA GOOSE—*Branta canadensis canadensis*

The Atlantic Canada goose nests primarily in eastern Labrador and Newfoundland, central Quebec, and Nova Scotia. Its wintering grounds overlap with the Todd's Canada goose, which is about the same size but a bit darker. This area extends from southern Nova Scotia to North Carolina. Estimates from sci-

*Atlantic race of Canada goose.*

entific survey show that the Atlantic Canada's population numbers more than 300,000 birds.

### Todd's Canada Goose—*Branta canadensis interior*

The Todd's race of goose is thought to be the most abundant of all eleven subspecies. A 1964 survey, conducted on the wintering grounds of the southeastern United States, showed that mixed flocks of Todd's and Atlantic's totaled nearly one million geese. Another survey concluded that *interior* equaled in numbers all of the other races combined.

These are fairly large, medium-colored birds weighing six to eleven pounds. Five distinct populations have been discovered in scattered areas from the Atlantic Ocean to the Rocky Mountains. The range map on page 61 shows these areas.

*The Todd's Canada goose—the most abundant of all races.*

**DUSKY CANADA GOOSE**—*Branta canadensis occidentalis*

The dusky Canada is one of the two large races of "dark" Canada geese. Its chocolate-brown plumage and somewhat restricted range make it relatively easy to distinguish, although it is often confused with the Vancouver race.

These birds nest off Alaska's southern coast and migrate close offshore on the way to their wintering grounds in the Willamette Valley of Oregon. An estimated twenty thousand dusky Canada geese exist.

**VANCOUVER CANADA GOOSE**—*Branta canadensis fulva*

This is the other large species of dark Canada goose. In size it is slightly larger than the dusky, weighing six to thirteen pounds.

The Vancouver goose is possibly the least migratory of all the Canadas since only about 10 per cent of their 20,000-member population moves away from the breeding grounds in winter. Most of the geese stay in the coastal area of southeastern Alaska southward along the coast of British Columbia. Those that do fly south overwinter in the Willamette Valley along with the dusky Canada geese.

SMALL CANADA GEESE

**CACKLING CANADA GOOSE**—*Branta canadensis minima*

As has been mentioned, the cackling goose is the smallest of all the subspecies. It has a distinctive, high-pitched call which it repeats time and again, accounting for its title of "cackler."

For such a small goose, no larger than a mallard duck, it has a long migration trip. Cacklers nest in a small region in western Alaska along the Bering Sea. In the fall they travel leisurely along the coast, stopping often to fatten themselves on tundra berries. By early October their travels have taken them along the Pacific Ocean to the mouth of the Columbia River. Here the tiny geese turn inland and follow the river through the

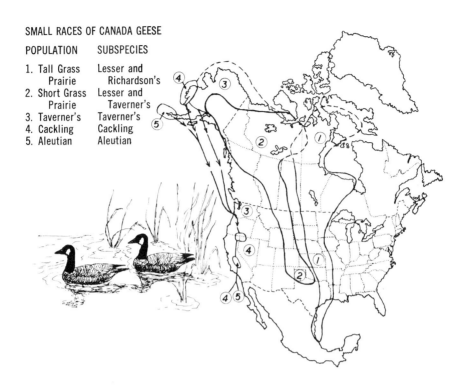

SMALL RACES OF CANADA GEESE

| POPULATION | SUBSPECIES |
|---|---|
| 1. Tall Grass Prairie | Lesser and Richardson's |
| 2. Short Grass Prairie | Lesser and Taverner's |
| 3. Taverner's | Taverner's |
| 4. Cackling | Cackling |
| 5. Aleutian | Aleutian |

Cascades and then southward to the Klamath Basin and north-eastern California. They linger there until late November when the migration continues to the Sacramento and San Joaquin regions and beyond.

Every once in awhile a few cacklers are forced from their normal migration path by bad weather and end up in such scattered areas as Baja California, Nevada, Wisconsin, Hawaii, and Japan.

Recent estimates place early fall populations of this race at 250,000 individuals.

RICHARDSON'S CANADA GOOSE—*Branta canadensis hutchinsii*

The Richardson's goose is the midwestern counterpart of the cackler although it is slightly larger and has a light chest and breast. It nests from the arctic coast directly southward to the

65

*The Richardson's goose was at one time called the Hutchin's goose.*

eastern edge of the Dakotas, Nebraska, and Kansas. Its winter home is far to the south in Oklahoma and the Gulf Coast of Texas and Mexico. Stragglers are occasionally seen in Ontario, Quebec, Maryland, and North Carolina.

**TAVERNER'S CANADA GOOSE**—*Branta canadensis taverneri*

The Taverner's goose ranges from 3½ to 5 pounds and is dark-plumaged.

These geese nest along the arctic coast of northwestern Canada and in western and northern Alaska. Most of the birds follow the Pacific coastline to winter in southcentral Washington and eastern Oregon, although a few can be found in the interior valleys of California and even west Texas. The Texas birds, however, most likely travel the Central Flyway to their wintering spots. Estimates of the Taverner's population size place its numbers at around 100,000.

*The Taverner's Canada goose is common in the Northwest.*

*The rare and endangered Aleutian Canada goose. A large white ring separates the neck and breast of these geese.*

**ALEUTIAN CANADA GOOSE**—*Branta canadensis leucopareia*

The Aleutian goose is about the same size as the Taverner's but differs somewhat in coloration. It is small but with a relatively large amount of white contrasting with the brown, forming a broken ring which separates its black neck from the breast.

Only a small portion of what may have once been a sizable population of these geese now remain. They nest on a few of the Aleutian Islands. In 1962 the manager of the Aleutian Islands National Wildlife Refuge discovered a flock of several hundred birds on the 6½-square-mile Buldir Island in the Aleutians.

Old records show that this goose once wintered along the coast of Washington and Oregon, in the interior California valleys, and south into Mexico. Some even migrated down the western side of the Pacific to Japan. Today, however, there are too few left to determine their winter range.

**LESSER CANADA GOOSE**—*Branta canadensis parvipes*

The lesser Canada is one of the smaller, light-colored races weighing in the area of six pounds.

Biologists cannot fully agree on the true classification of geese assigned to this subspecies since there is great variation in their range. Typically, though, they nest inland in scattered spots across the Northwest territories of Canada and central and eastern Alaska. Depending on their exact nest sites, they follow well-defined migration routes to their wintering grounds in Oklahoma, Texas, Mexico, and California.

Since the lesser Canadas intermingle with Richardson's geese in their southern wintering areas, it is impossible to determine exact numbers of each. Surveys of these spots, however, may turn up anywhere from 200,000 to 300,000 birds in an average year.

### Snow goose—*Chen caerulescens*

The lesser and greater snow geese are similar to some of the races of Canada geese in that they are alike in habits and physical features but seldom come in contact with one another.

The greater snow goose of the East is somewhat larger than, but otherwise identical to, the lesser snow goose of the West. Although their geographic ranges are quite different, their life histories are very much the same. The lesser snow goose also has a dark color phase which is known as a "blue goose." These darker birds tend to stay together and form distinct flocks with

*A flock of greater snow geese at Brigantine National Wildlife Refuge in New Jersey. Note the Atlantic City skyline in the background.*

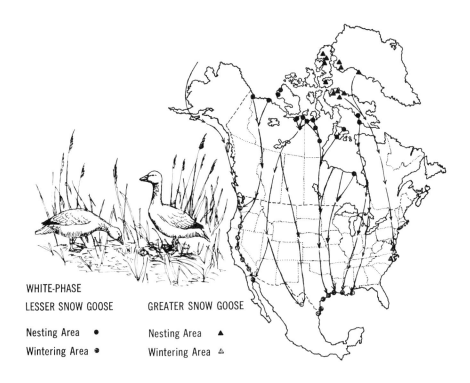

WHITE-PHASE
LESSER SNOW GOOSE          GREATER SNOW GOOSE

Nesting Area    ●          Nesting Area    ▲
Wintering Area  ◉          Wintering Area  △

a different range than the white birds. The greater snow goose
has no other color phase.

There's no greater thrill than to observe a flock of three or
four thousand of these magnificent white birds winging southward with the approaching winter. Yet, despite the bird's relatively large populations, snow goose numbers are only a fraction
as great as they were in the mid-1800s. During this time the snow
goose was a very naive and trusting creature. Since they nested
in places inaccessible to man, most of the geese had never heard
the shot of a gun and had little fear of the first ones they witnessed during their migratory travels. As it was, meat hunters
could literally walk or ride through the flocks, shooting or killing them with clubs.

One early writer gives an account of the mass slaughter. He
writes that the snow geese "often cover so densely with their

masses the plains in the vicinity of the marshes as to give the ground the appearance of being clothed in snow. Easily approached on horseback, the natives sometimes near them in this manner, then suddenly putting spurs to their animals, gallop into the flock, striking to the right and left with short clubs, and trampling them beneath their horses' feet. I have known a native to procure seventeen birds in a single charge of this kind through a flock covering several acres."

This sort of uncontrolled killing continued until 1918 when the Migratory Bird Treaty finally afforded the birds some protection. And although they will probably never achieve the great numbers of their ancestors, the modern snow geese, particularly the lesser race, continue to prosper throughout their range.

The snow goose's former scientific species name of *hyperborea* hinted at the place where they breed—"beyond the north wind." It is here, within the Arctic Circle, that the snow goose raises its family each summer. Only one other species of goose, the American brant, nests farther north than the lesser snow goose.

Nesting as they do in regions where few men dwell, very little is actually known about the snow's breeding and nesting habits. What is known is based largely on the reports of Eskimos and from studies of captive specimens.

Like other geese, it is thought that the snow goose mates for life. Original pairings are done on the bird's wintering grounds with males threatening one another and occasional battles breaking out.

Of all the geese, snows seem to be the most gregarious. Even at nesting time they like to be close to one another. In one northern tundra area there are recorded concentrations of 1,200 pairs to the square mile, although the average density is certainly much smaller.

70

*Snow geese arrive at their breeding grounds in early June.*

In the eastern portions of their breeding grounds, the snow geese arrive in early June and begin to nest within two weeks. To the west they arrive the last week in May and get a one-week jump on the season. It usually takes about eleven days for the entire clutch of seven or eight eggs to be laid. The nest seems quite simple when compared to swans and certain other geese, since a slight depression in the ground is all that is needed. Little vegetation is used although the female is quite liberal with donations of soft, white down from her breast.

In some instances incubation may be carried out by both parents although, regardless of the male's help, he stays in the immediate vicinity of the nest as a faithful guard during the entire 28-day incubation period. By mid-August, about six weeks after hatching, the goslings are able to make their first flights.

Wherever there are great concentrations of nesting birds, there will also be a variety of predators seeking their share. The birds which nest earliest get their choice of the prime nest sites—in good cover or alongside water and away from the regular routes of the arctic fox and Eskimos who collect the eggs for food. Gulls, parasitic jaegers, and ravens also take the eggs, particularly when they are left uncovered and the parents are away from the nest.

The bulk of the snow goose's diet consists of vegetable matter since, like the Canada goose, it is a grazing bird. Although cul-

71

*Note the "grinning patch" on this blue-phase lesser snow goose.*

tivated grains such as barley, wheat, and rice are favored, they also eat the seeds of aquatic plants. The young feed ravenously on the insects and their larvae which abound in the arctic potholes during the summer. This rich protein diet promotes the rapid growth necessary for the youngsters to achieve flight stage before the arrival of early winter snows. All yearling geese can be distinguished from the adults by their sooty gray coats which do not turn white until the following summer.

The adult snow goose is completely white except for its black *primaries* (the outermost flight feathers) and pink bill and feet. All snow geese have what is called a *grinning patch*, a small area between the mandibles where the lamellae are exposed. This gives an observer the impression that the geese are smiling.

Those who have witnessed the immense strings of snow geese pouring out of the sky like a winter blizzard and singing their high-pitched songs find it difficult to believe that the flocks were ever any greater than they are today. Although man was the villain a hundred years back, today he is their chief benefactor. Without the many refuges open to wintering flocks and the protection offered them through modern hunting laws, the snow goose could well have suffered the plight of the trumpeter swan.

## LESSER SNOW GOOSE—*Chen caerulescens caerulescens*

It wasn't until 1973 that the American Ornithologists' Union finally declared that the white lesser snow goose and the blue goose were actually the same species of bird. Up until that time the blue goose was considered a separate species which was known to frequently interbreed with the lesser snow.

Two things had confused the biologists. For one, the blue goose only interbreeds with the lesser subspecies, never the greater. Secondly, although blues are frequently found with the white geese, most of them form flocks with separate breeding and wintering ranges.

After a detailed study, biologists decided that both geese had very similar physical features—only their feather colors were different. They also discovered that the geese tended to choose mates similar in color to one of the parents. Because of this, the two color phases formed separate flocks in slightly different areas of the continent.

BLUE-PHASE LESSER SNOW GOOSE

Nesting Area
Wintering Area

The average lesser subspecies has a body length of about thirty inches and a wingspan double that. It weighs three to six pounds.

The Cree Indians refer to this goose as "wa-wa" (Indian for "goose") or "wavey." The white birds are known as "little waveys" or "white brants" while the darker birds are called "blue waveys."

Of the white snow geese, the lesser variety is far more common than the greater. It breeds along the Arctic Coast, nesting in fourteen major concentration areas between Baffin Island and Siberia. Winters find them migrating in massive flocks to wintering grounds in California and along the Gulf Coast from Texas to Florida.

The blue goose nests in tundra country along the western edge of Baffin Island as well as around Hudson Bay and near the Perry River in the Northwest Territories.

In winter the blue goose migrates directly southward to the coasts of Louisiana, Texas, and Mexico. Here flocks of blue-phase and white-phase birds intermingle. In southwestern Louisiana the blue geese now outnumber the white ones and their populations seem to be increasing in the West.

*The classification of the blue goose—the dark phase of the lesser snow goose—confused scientists. It was considered a separate species for many years.*

*Two greater snow geese fly in unison.*

The blue's spring migration covers about three thousand miles and takes eleven weeks to complete. Oddly enough, their fall journey is about six hundred miles shorter, since they follow a more direct route.

The characteristic markings of the blue goose—a bluish-gray body with white head and neck—make it easy to identify. Pink legs and feet and a conspicuous grinning patch on the beak complete its dress. The white-phase goose is identical to the greater snow goose except for its smaller size.

Even though the only major physical difference between these birds is their coloration, they are surprisingly different. It is easy to understand why scientists had such a difficult time in determining their relationship.

**GREATER SNOW GOOSE**—*Chen caerulescens atlantica*

As its subspecies name implies, the greater snow goose dwells where its lesser cousin's range ends. During spring migrations, practically all of the greater snow geese in North America take a rest stop at Cap Tourmente on the St. Lawrence River about thirty miles south of Quebec City. Here they linger for eight to ten weeks before heading south to the Chesapeake Bay-Currituck Sound area of Maryland, Virginia, and North Carolina. In winter they can be seen at Brigantine, Bombay Hook, Blackwater, Pea Island, and Chincoteague National Wildlife Refuges. In the spring these geese again gather at Cap Tourmente before heading northward in massive flocks to their summer home.

The nesting grounds of the greater subspecies partly overlap those of the lesser and includes the region south and west of Baffin Bay and western Greenland. Even though they come in contact with the two lesser versions of the snow, the greater subspecies does not interbreed with either of them.

### WHITE-FRONTED GOOSE—*Anser albifrons*

This is the goose that hunters have nicknamed "specklebelly." Some, however, know it as the "gray wavey," "tiger brant," or "laughing goose." The latter name comes from its loud, squealing *wah-wah-wah-wah* call, described by some as a sort of wild laughter.

The white-front is truly a western species. Seldom does it roam east of the Mississippi, for it prefers the arctic prairies in summer and the open vistas of California, Texas, and Mexico in winter.

It is the white "front," or face, of this goose from which its name is derived. A narrow band of white covers the entire forepart of the head and has even been included in the make-up of its Latin scientific name *albifrons* (*albus* meaning white and *frons* indicating the forehead). The title of specklebelly is also quite descriptive since the breast and belly are grayish-white with irregular splashes of brownish-black throughout. Yellow feet and a pink bill complete the colors on this common western waterfowl.

To the nature lover the call of the specklebelly signals the coming of autumn, for it often arrives on its California wintering grounds in September—long before the other arctic-breeders show up.

76

WHITE-FRONTED GOOSE

Nesting Area ■
Migration Stops ⦂•⦂
Wintering Area ▨

Right: *The white-fronted goose is known to sportsmen as the "speckle-belly."* Left: *The white on the forepart of the head gives the white-fronted goose his name.*

Its breeding grounds are scattered over 2,500 miles of Canadian and Alaskan tundra. Here, in the "land of the midnight sun," the white-fronts stake out territories in which to nest and feed. During the last week of May and into early June the females scratch out bowl-shaped nests which are then lined with grasses, mosses, and down. Four to seven eggs are laid over the period of a week or two and incubated, by the female alone, for four weeks. The gander stays nearby, guarding both his mate and the eggs from predators. Although the eggs are a buff-white color when laid, the mud brought back to the nest on the feet and feathers of the female soon stains them brown.

The goslings are hatched in a coat of olive-colored down. Shortly thereafter, they are led on their first trek through the wet tundra in search of insects and insect larvae as well as grasses and sedges.

When the goslings are about two weeks old, the parents begin their molt and are flightless for a period of about three weeks. During this time some adult birds are captured by the natives of the north country for food. Although it may seem cruel to some, the numbers taken are relatively small and are certainly a welcome change of diet to the Eskimos and Indians that live on fish, seal meat, and blubber most of the time.

The white-fronts are considered the finest of all geese as table-fare. This, along with their migration schedule and pattern, exposes them to human and animal predators most of the year. In addition to the Eskimos and Indians, Americans hunt them in the fall and Mexicans in winter. Besides disease, parasites, and accidents, jaegers, skuas, gulls, ravens, and foxes also take their toll throughout the summer.

Yet, despite this constant predation on the specklebellies, their populations are sizable. Between 90,000 and 120,000 are taken by hunters in southern Canada and the United States annually. Adding this to the hunting and predation in the north plus the natural losses due to disease, weather, and accidents, one must marvel at their annual nesting success.

The birds often start north while the ponds and sloughs are still covered with ice, as if impatient to begin their nesting duties. Traveling in large flocks, an old, experienced gander leads the noisy army at a steady forty to fifty mile-per-hour pace, high above the ground. And even after they have disappeared from view, their laughter still filters back as a reminder of their passage and with the promise of a successful spring.

There are actually four subspecies of white-fronted geese, although only three of them are typically North American. The common white-fronted is the most numerous. A darker Greenland subspecies winters in Ireland, England, and Wales, although a few may make their way down the east coast to Quebec and into the United States. The lesser white-fronted goose is found in northern Eurasia and never in North America.

### COMMON WHITE-FRONTED GOOSE—*Anser albifrons albifrons*

The common specklebelly achieves a length of 2½ feet and a wingspread of 5 feet. The male weighs about 5½ pounds, with the female being slightly smaller. Its breeding range covers the northern half of Alaska, the Yukon, and the Northwest Territories of Canada and the southern Greenland coast.

This race typically travels and feeds in large flocks, often setting down on a field of wheat, barley, or rice and causing considerable damage.

### TULE GOOSE—*Anser albifrons gambelli*

A variation in habits and certain other characteristics has accounted for the classification of the tule goose as a separate subspecies. Except for its larger size (about 30 per cent larger) and a darker plumage, however, it looks very much like *Anser albifrons albifrons*.

A cloak of mystery surrounds the tule goose. Scientists have searched the Canadian north for their breeding grounds but have only found one region along the Perry River where they nest. In winter they gather in the central valleys of northern California.

The tule geese travel in smaller flocks than their smaller cousins and are not nearly as wary. They often approach hunters' decoys without first investigating and are prone to fly low over the ground.

Scientists fear for the survival of this race of goose since fewer reports of it come in each year. The tule prefers the open water of ponds and sloughs surrounded by tules (a type of bulrush) and willows and not the open uplands and grain fields favored by the more common race. Seldom do the two races mingle with one another, even when they are on the same breeding grounds in the north.

### BRANT—*Branta bernicla*

Even scientists can't agree on whether the American brant and the black brant are two separate species or merely subspecies. For our purpose, we will follow the more up-to-date references that classify them as subspecies.

Both races are very similar in appearance. They measure two feet in length, have a four-foot wingspread, and weigh about three pounds. The American brant, also known as the Atlantic brant, has a black head, neck, breast, and tail. The jet black neck is broken up only by a partial white ring with black streaks. Its belly is a mottled gray-white. The black brant, known also as the Pacific brant, is almost identical except for the more complete neck band and a much blacker belly.

As their alternate names (Atlantic and Pacific) may indicate, both birds are "sea geese." Although their breeding grounds overlap and they are known to interbreed occasionally, the

AMERICAN BRANT

Nesting Area ▲▲▲

Wintering Area ▦

BLACK BRANT

Nesting Area ♣●

Wintering Area ▨

separate races winter far from one another along the Atlantic and Pacific coasts.

By the end of April most brant are headed for their summer homes in the Alaskan and Canadian north. By the beginning of June they are on the breeding grounds where they immediately search for suitable nest sites on small islands and along the coast-lines of the larger arctic islands. From the moment they arrive until the time when their families can take wing, the brant are plagued by predators. Snowy owls and wolves may take both young and adults, while jaegers, gulls, arctic foxes, and even grizzly bears search out nests and feed on the eggs. The glaucous gull, largest of the arctic's gulls, feeds on the young brant in some regions, swallowing the downy youngsters whole.

Brant nest only a foot or so above the high tide line. Their simple nest consists of nothing more than a hollow depression lined with down and a few bits of seaweed, mosses, or lichens. Since they need not choose and fight for mates upon arrival, the females are ready to lay their eggs within a few days. If cold weather has not completely left the tundra and nesting is delayed, the females begin to resorb the eggs within their bodies and have smaller clutches—or none at all—as the season progresses. A delayed season would not allow the goslings adequate time to grow or time for the adults to molt before freeze-up. Geese that fail to nest begin to molt almost immediately, not after the incubation period's equivalent.

Successful nests typically contain three to five eggs that undergo a four-week incubation. While the female sits on the eggs, the gander must be ever-alert for the numerous marauding gulls and jaegers overhead.

Soon after the dark brown goslings hatch, they are hurried to the sea where they are immediately able to swim and dive. In the tide flats they feed on insects, larvae, grasses, and tundra blossoms. Within seven weeks they can fly. At this time they congregate in large flocks wherever plenty of food is available. By early September they are heading south, to overwinter along both coasts of the United States.

*The American brant and the black brant are considered as the same species by some scientists and as separate ones by others.*

*A flock of American or Atlantic brant.*

Seldom does one see individual pairs of brant, for they are strongly social in nature. They even nest in colonies and sometimes pool their offspring for greater protection.

### AMERICAN BRANT—*Branta bernicla hrota*

This is the only sea goose of the Atlantic Coast and is rarely found any distance from salt water. In flight it is readily recognizable, even at a distance. The long wavy lines of dark geese gradually show contrasts between the dark head and neck and the white underparts as the birds come closer. In true goose fashion, the brant continually call among themselves as they speed along their offshore routes.

In winter, the American brant can be found from Cape Cod south to North Carolina. Brigantine National Wildlife Refuge, within sight of Atlantic City, attracts great concentrations of these sea geese each fall. Most of the 225,000 birds now in existence come to rest there at one time or another.

In the early 1930s, however, the eastern brant's population was at a dangerous low and the bird was on the verge of extinction. Its main food, eelgrass, suddenly contracted a disease and

83

died off, with the subsequent demise of the brant. Eelgrass composed about 90 per cent of the brant's winter diet at that time.

Fortunately, the surviving birds changed their food habits and their numbers gradually rose. With the change, the birds also lost their desirability as game birds, since their substitute diet of sea lettuce also changed the sweet flavor of the flesh. Today, though, eelgrass is slowly recovering and the brant are again feeding on it.

Strangely enough, with the change in their food also came a change in their spring migration routes. No longer dependent on the eelgrass which grew along the coast, they used overland routes for their flights north and continue to use them today.

Atlantic brant nest on the eastern arctic coastlines and islands where, in the westernmost parts, they raise families in the company of their Pacific cousins.

### BLACK BRANT—*Branta bernicla nigricans*

The eelgrass on the Pacific Coast was little affected by the strange disease almost half a century back and consequently the black brant hasn't noticeably changed its habits since that time.

On their northerly flights the brant still follow the Pacific shoreline until they reach the Yukon where they scatter east and west to seek their nesting spots. The following autumn they return along a similar route to spend the winter from Washington south to Baja California. Some brant also nest along the coast of eastern Siberia and winter in China and Japan.

### Ross' GOOSE—*Chen rossii*

The tiny Ross' goose holds the questionable distinction of being the rarest goose in North America. It may also rank as the smallest, since it is of about the same size as the cackling Canada goose. It averages two feet in length, has a 50-inch wingspan, and weighs only 2¾ pounds.

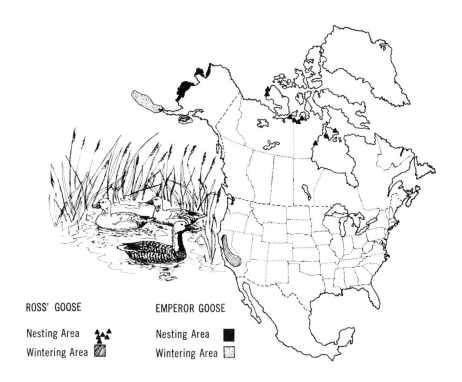

ROSS' GOOSE

Nesting Area ▲▲▲
Wintering Area ▨

EMPEROR GOOSE

Nesting Area ■
Wintering Area ▧

*Chen rossii* looks like a miniature snow goose. It is completely white except for the black primary feathers which, like the snow goose, are more noticeable in flight than on the water. Its bill has a salmon-pink hue but without the snow's distinctive grinning patch. A series of well-developed bumps or warts covers the base of the upper mandible. Its feet are similar to the bill in coloration.

Until 1938 the Ross' goose was known only as a waterfowl that wintered in the California valleys, migrated north through Oregon, Washington, and Alberta, and then disappeared into the vast northland tundra. In that year the manager of a Hudson's Bay Company post discovered some Ross' geese nesting in the Perry River region of the Northwest Territories. The bird had been first described in 1861 and named for Bernard Ross, chief factor of the Hudson's Bay Company, who had collected

85

*Ross' geese.*

some specimens. It was another seventy-seven years before anymore was known about this diminutive and mysterious bird.

Almost the entire winter population of Ross' geese, which number about thirty thousand individuals, spends the colder seasons in the interior valleys of California. Occasional wanderers are found in Louisiana and Texas in the company of snow and blue geese.

In early March the Ross' geese begin a slow, steady northward migration. Depending on a particular year's weather and snow cover, they arrive at their nesting grounds during the last week of May and begin nesting chores during the second week of June.

Both the nest structure, except for its smaller size, and the method of raising the young are identical to that of the lesser snow goose. Built of willow twigs and lined with mosses, grasses, and down, the nest shelters four or five eggs. Incubation, performed by the female, takes from twenty-one to twenty-four days.

Plagued by the typical tundra predators, Ross' goose families gather along the marshy edges of lakes or float downstream

86

toward the coast. Here the goslings grow quickly on insects and the tender shoots of sedges and grasses. By late August the young can fly and September finds them moving south, leaving the northland earlier than most other geese except for, perhaps, the white-fronts.

*Rossii* is a very docile and somewhat tame goose as compared to other species. In years past, market hunters took advantage of this personality trait by slaughtering them in large numbers to be sold commercially in California. Although at one time they were protected from hunting in Canada and the United States, the law was ineffective because they were so easily mistaken for the legal snow geese. In recent years, however, hunting for "white geese" on the Pacific and Central flyways was set back to early October. It was discovered that by this time most of the Ross' geese had already migrated through and were safe from gunning.

During the winter the Ross' goose feeds on wild oats, barley, and grass, keeping up a noisy *luk-luk* gabble throughout the day.

### EMPEROR GOOSE—*Philacte canagica*

The emperor goose is thought by many to be the most handsome and definitely the least known of resident North American geese. Its breeding grounds are only a few hundred miles from the wintering grounds, making long migratory flights unnecessary and further adding to its seclusion.

Even though the emperor is considered to be a poor table bird due to its fishy taste, Eskimos take great numbers of them during their flightless periods, often driving them into enclosures where they are killed. The natives also raid their nests and gather eggs, making this bird important as a food source of the northwest people. Gulls, jaegers, foxes, and owls take an additional toll of eggs and young.

The name *Philacte* is well chosen, for literally translated from

*The emperor goose is probably the most handsome and least known of all North American geese.*

Greek it means "lover of the seashore"—the very place where this goose spends most of its life. The young are raised along the arctic and Bering coasts of Alaska and Siberia. Winter finds the greatest North American concentrations in the Aleutian Islands, although stragglers are occasionally observed in British Columbia and California.

The emperor's blue-gray suit is marked with crescents of black and white. The head and back of the neck are white, contrasted by the jet black throat. A white tail and bright orange feet complete its dress.

The emperors leave the Aleutians in late April and arrive on the breeding grounds during the first two weeks of May. Most clutches of five or six eggs are completed in early June and incubated for twenty-four days. Unlike most ganders, the male emperor does not accompany the female during this period but instead combs the nearby beaches for food. By the time the goslings hatch, however, he is back on the job. The parents take the youngsters away from the nest to feed on aquatic insects and marsh grasses, later moving away from the shore to feed on upland grasses and berries.

By early August the adults have grown new plumage and the

88

young have gained their flight wings. Migration begins the first week in September and before long they are back on their wintering grounds in the Aleutians.

The bulk of the emperor's diet is animal matter, which accounts for the tainted flavor of its meat. Shellfish and crustaceans are gleaned along the tidal flats and supplemented by grasses, cranberries, and mossberries.

Despite their many human and animal predators, emperor populations today number about 200,000. Since it stays far from the centers of human population, however, sportsmen and naturalists seldom get to see this beautiful representative of the waterfowl world.

**BARNACLE GOOSE**—*Branta leucopsis*

According to an ancient Norwegian belief, the first appearance of the barnacle goose was thought to be in the shell of a barnacle (a mollusk that attaches itself to rocks, ship bottoms, driftwood, and so on). From this fable sprang the goose's name.

*Branta leucopsis* makes its summer home in northeastern

*The barnacle goose nests in Greenland.*

Greenland and departs for Europe in the fall, migrating in the opposite direction from our other native geese. They are quite common on the west coast of Scotland in winter.

On the ledges and cliffs of the rugged Greenland coast, the female barnacle goose lays four or five grayish eggs while the gander stands guard against predators. When the goslings hatch they are faced with as much as a 1,500-foot descent to the streams and ponds below. Buoyed by strong updrafts of wind, the youngsters alternately climb and tumble down the bluffs. Parents occasionally help out by carrying the youngsters in their bills and one account even describes an adult flying down to the water with a gosling on its back.

Much like the brant in shape and appearance, the barnacle goose is distinguished by a white head with a black crown blending into a black neck and chest. A small black mask covers the eyes behind the upper mandible. The remainder of its body is gray above and whitish below.

Their calls have been described as sounding "like a pack of terriers." In the fall a few barnacle geese may straggle down the east coast where they thrill the birdwatchers who are on hand to sight these strange visitors from the north.

# 6. Swans, Geese, and Man

### IN EARLIER TIMES

Swans and geese have long attracted the attentions of man. By their sheer beauty and the mysteries of their migrations, they have stimulated songs and stories throughout the centuries.

In Greek mythology the swan was thought to have unique powers enabling it to foretell the future. Many stories give accounts of the swan's habit of singing just before death, hence the expression "swan song." Legends of "swan maidens" have been written, describing the ways in which beautiful girls were clothed in the dress of swans, and shed their cloaks only in the wooded haunts of secluded lakes and streams. In one story a prince rode the back of a swan maiden that he had fallen in love with.

*Cygnus the Swan* is the name given to a northern constellation in the Milky Way. (It is also known as the Northern Cross.) Various Greek myths describe the way *Cygnus* appeared in the sky, with his wings outspread and his long neck pointing southward.

The primitive people first saw the swan as a source of food but as time went on, later civilizations associated its whiteness, gracefulness, and size with aesthetic and spiritual symbols.

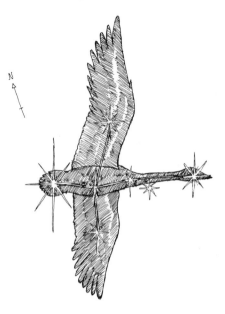

*Cygnus the Swan is the name given to a northern constellation in the Milky Way.*

In England the mute swan is regarded as a royal bird and no subject can own it except by grant from the Crown. Every year captive flocks are taken from the water in a ceremony known as "swan-upping" and a "swan-mark" is cut into the upper mandible of the youngest birds to distinguish their ownership.

Geese, too, have been important and popular over the years, although not in the same fashion as swans. Early white settlers were familiar with the fowl of their native lands and welcomed the wild geese as food and as providers for their warm feather beds and pillows. "Goose grease" was used in cooking and also as a medication for everything from colds to rheumatism.

Today the wild geese are symbols of freedom and wildness. Since they spend winters near civilization and migrate above towns and cities during their annual journeys, the wild geese accompany the robin and the early wildflowers as harbingers of spring.

### MANAGEMENT AND CONTROL

Compared to other gamebirds such as the grouse, quail, and pheasant, waterfowl are relatively difficult to manage. Most swans, geese, and ducks travel thousands of miles each year and must find suitable habitat wherever they happen to be throughout the seasons.

Waterfowl from the northern Canadian and Alaskan breeding grounds travel to all the states, the Provinces of Canada, and into Mexico. Organizations such as Ducks Unlimited, with chapters in Canada, Mexico, and the United States, have donated millions of dollars for the restoration, preservation, and creation of nesting habitats for all waterfowl in the Canadian Prairie regions. By 1980 Ducks Unlimited hopes to have leased over 6½ million acres of these "waterfowl factories." It is just as important, however, to ensure adequate wintering grounds with sufficient amounts of food as it is to conserve the nesting territories in the north country.

The United States Fish and Wildlife Service, a governmental agency, undertakes regular migratory fowl surveys so that up-to-the-minute decisions can be made regarding the hunting and protection of all species. Through their National Wildlife Refuge System, more than 30 million acres in forty-six states now provide rest stops and wintering grounds for all waterfowl. Funds

*Much research is being done today to assure continued success for all waterfowl. These Aleutian geese are being reared at Patuxent Wildlife Research Center under the care of U.S. Fish and Wildlife Service biologists.*

from Migratory Bird Hunting Stamps, purchased by all United States hunters for waterfowl shooting, are used to purchase and maintain these refuges.

Although the plights of the trumpeter swan, Ross' goose, American brant, and others have been outlined in these pages, our waterfowl populations today are healthy. Back in the 1930s, when drought and wetland destruction reduced populations to their lowest ever, a new concern for all of our wildfowl came into being. Since then biologists, naturalists, and sportsmen alike have donated their money and time to the common cause of ensuring the continued survival of every species of waterfowl.

## For the Future

All things considered, the future of North America's swans and geese is bright. As long as their breeding grounds remain unmolested and the march of civilization does not remove valuable wetlands, present populations should continue to prosper. Never before has so much knowledge been accumulated and scientifically analyzed. We are equipped now to make studies and decisions regarding wildfowl that benefit both man and bird.

If we had been as farsighted seventy-five years ago as we are today, perhaps the problems of habitat loss and general lack of concern for wildlife would not be here to haunt us now. A future human population of 300 million by the year 2000 is predicted. Automation, increased food production, and the need for more living space and leisure-time activities are inevitable. The choice is ours. We can either ignore the wild creatures or make them an integral part of our planning. Whether our children and grandchildren will still be able to seek the wild swans and thrill to the calls of great flocks of geese pouring in from the north depends on us—and the value we place on our wildfowl neighbors.

94

# Bibliography

Bent, Arthur C. *Life Histories of North American Wildfowl.* Vol. 2. New York: Dover Publications, Inc., 1925.

Johnsgard, Paul A. *Waterfowl: Their Biology and Natural History.* Lincoln: University of Nebraska Press, 1968.

Kortright, Francis H. *The Ducks, Geese and Swans of North America.* Harrisburg, Pa.: The Stackpole Company, 1953.

Linduska, Joseph P., ed. *Waterfowl Tomorrow.* Washington, D.C.: U.S. Department of the Interior, 1964.

Rue, Leonard L. *Game Birds of North America.* New York: Harper and Row, 1974.

Van Wormer, Joe. *The World of the Canada Goose.* Philadelphia: J. B. Lippincott Company, 1968.

———. *The World of the Swan.* Philadelphia: J. B. Lippincott Company, 1972.

Wetmore, Alexander. *Water, Prey and Game Birds of North America.* Washington, D.C.: National Geographic Society, 1965.

# Index

(Page numbers in **boldface** are those on which illustrations appear)

Anatidae, 9, 10
Anserinae, 10
Audubon, John James, 34
Banding, 30, **31**
Barnacle goose, 10, **89**–90
Bill structure, 16, **17**, 41
Blue goose. *See* Snow goose, lesser
Brant, 10, 31, 33, 52, 80–84
  American, 17, 28, 70, 80, **82**, **83**–84, 94
  black, 17, 28, 80, **82**, 84
Brigantine National Wildlife Refuge, 68, 83
Canada goose, 10, 11, 12, 13, 17, 18, 21–**22**, **23**–24, 25, 26, 27–28, 31, 32, 33, 50, **51**, 52–68
  Races: Aleutian, **67**, 93; Atlantic, 62, 63; cackling, 11, 12, 58, 64–65; dusky, 64; giant, 11, 27, 58, **61**; lesser, 67–68; Richardson's, 62, 65–66; Taverner's, **66**; Todd's, 52, **63**; Vancouver, 64; western, **62**
Care of young, 27–28, **54**, 56–58
Chesapeake Bay, 23, 43, 75
Color phases, 17, 68–69
Cygnets, 38, **39**–40, 43, **44**, 48
Cygninae, 10
Cygnus the Swan, 91, **92**
Displaying, 21–**22**
Ducks, 9–10, 22, 25, 53
Ducks Unlimited, 93
Eggs, **26**–27, **38**, 43, 48, 55–56, 71, 78, 82, 86, 87, 90
Emperor goose, 10, 87–89
Feeding, 22, **23**, **24**, 39–40, 43, 49, 58–59, 71–72, 82, 83–84, 87, 88
Flight, 31–33, **40**, 44–45, 53–54, 59
Flyways, **28**–30, 51
Geese. *See* individual species
Goslings, 12, **56**–58, 78, 87
Hazards, 18–**20**, 39, 44
Hunting, 41–42, 51, 69, 78
Hybrids, 17

Longevity, 17–**18**
Management, 92–**93**
Mating, 24–25, 49, 54, 70
Migration, **28**–31, 53–54, 71, 86, 88, 89, 90
Migratory Bird Treaties, 10, 34, 36, 51, 70
Molting, **12**–13, 36, 44, 70
Mute swan, 10, 14, **18**, 21, 25, 26, 28–29, 45–**49**
Nesting, 25–26, **37**, 42–43, 47, 54–55, 70–71, 78, 81–82, 86, 87, 90
Patuxent Wildlife Research Center, 31, 93
Physical features: bill structure, 16, **17**, 41; coloration, 11–12; feet and legs, 15–16; hearing, 14, 15; plumage, 11–12, **45**, 58; sight, 14–15; size, 11, 45; sound production, 13–14, 37, 44; weight, 11
Predators, 20, 39, 55–56, 57, 71, 78, 81, 82, 86, 87
Red Rock Lakes National Wildlife Refuge, 36, 37, 40
Ross' goose, 10, 11, 12, 33, 51, 84–87, 94
Snow goose, 10, 17, 31, 33, 50, **68**–76
  greater, **29**, **68**, 69, **75**–76
  lesser, 68, 73–75
    blue-phase, 17, 18, 68–69, **72**, 73–75
Species and subspecies, 52
Swans. *See* individual species
Territories, 25, 28, 54–55
Trumpeter swan, 9, 12, 14, 18, 22, 25, **26**, 32, 33, 34, 36–40, 46, 94
U.S. Fish and Wildlife Service, **93**–94
Whistling swan, 10, 14, 20, 23, 25, 26–27, 29, 32, 33, 34, **41**–**45**, 46
White-fronted goose, 10, **13**, 18, 28, 33, 52, 76–80
  common, 79
  Greenland, 79
  lesser, 79
  tule, 79–80

36218

J
598  F
FEGELY
    WONDERS  OF  GEESE  AND
SWANS                    4.95

7